Weighing up the E

HOW AND WHY:

The Russian Revolution

Elizabeth Campling

Dryad Press Limited London

Contents

ACKNOWLEDGMENTS
The author and publishers would like to thank the following for their permission to reproduce illustrations:
BBC Hulton Picture Library, page 44; The Illustrated London News Picture Library, pages 32, 36, 38; Novosti Press Agency, pages 8 (top), 11, 16, 19, 24, 27, 29, 45, 47, 50, 52; The Elsie Timbey Collection, Society for Cultural Relations with the USSR, for the pictures on the front cover: Lenin on his way to Petrograd; an anti-Bolshevik poster, "Russia sacrificed on the altar of the International"; and the decree of peace.

© Elizabeth Campling 1986   First published 1986
Typeset by Tek-Art Ltd, Kent
and printed in Great Britain by R J Acford Ltd, Chichester, Sussex
for the Publishers, Dryad Press Limited,
4 Fitzhardinge Street, London W1H 0AH

Introduction

There were two revolutions in Russia in 1917. The "February Revolution" (8-16 March) overthrew the centuries-old Tsarist autocracy and replaced it with a "Provisional Government", pledged to establish full political democracy throughout the country and to arrange for the election of a Constituent Assembly. The function of this assembly would be to decide on a *permanent* form of government for post-Tsarist Russia, after which the Provisional Government would step down. Eight months later, before the Constituent Assembly could even be elected, the "October Revolution" (6-7 November) brought a Bolshevik (Communist) regime to power.

For those of us born after these events, there may seem something natural or inevitable about Communist rule in Russia, but it is only with the benefit of hindsight that we see the October Revolution as a turning point in history. The study of history is, in fact, a highly selective process. Out of the billions of events that make up the fabric of the past, the ones we choose to examine are those which turn out to be successful in changing the course of human affairs, and it is not always obvious until long afterwards exactly which those are. Few contemporaries, including some of the more pessimistic Bolsheviks, dreamt that the new government would last for more than a few weeks, and, indeed, it was not until 1921, after three years of devastating civil war, that Bolshevik control was firmly established over most of the former Tsarist Empire.

If we are to understand why the Bolsheviks came to power, we cannot altogether avoid some discussion of why Tsarism collapsed in the first place, for the problems that bedevilled the old regime did not automatically disappear just because a revolution had taken place. Nevertheless, against the background of the First World War, the February Revolution was hardly surprising. The same cannot be said about the October Revolution. The Bolsheviks had been a tiny and largely disregarded group in March 1917, and that they should sweep into power eight months later was something few observers would have deemed credible. It is to an analysis of events between March and October 1917 that the bulk of this book will be devoted.

The key for unlocking a particular event in the past is to understand why the people involved – both individuals and groups – behaved as they did. This is not as simple as it sounds. No one approaches events without bringing with him or her a great deal of mental "baggage" – preconceived ideas based on the hopes, fears, ambitions and prejudices accumulated during his or her lifetime. Consciously or sub-consciously, people interpret what goes on around them in the light of these pre-conceptions, and this, in turn, dictates how they react to them. It is the historian's job to evaluate these reactions and grade them according to their importance in deciding the final outcome.

This book is a reconstruction of eight months in 1917 as experienced by the people involved. It looks at how and why they reacted to events and

The dating of events in the revolutionary period

In 1917 Russia still used the Julian calendar, which had long been abandoned elsewhere, and in this period Russian dates run thirteen days behind those used in the rest of Europe. The Communist Government brought Russia into line with the West in 1918. To avoid confusion, the dating used throughout this book has been standardized and the modern calendar used. Thus we say that the first revolution began on 8 March, rather than 23 February; the Bolshevik coup took place on the night of 6/7 November, rather than 24/25 October. However, because the terms "February Revolution" and "October Revolution" were so widely used by contemporaries, these have been retained.

how the sum total of their reactions contributed to the final result, although no one could be sure of the complete shape until the last piece of the jigsaw had been fitted. The short biographies beginning on page 62, giving the backgrounds and views of some of the key figures of the revolutionary year, constitute, therefore, an essential part of the book and are intended to help you judge how much weight to place on each piece of evidence.

Little has been said so far about facts and dates, the stuff of which many people believe that history is made. Facts and figures are the essential bare bones of history but on their own they do not explain much. It is how people interpret and react to the "facts" that provides history's motivating force. In this book we shall discover examples of events — the July Days and the Kornilov Affair are two of them — where it is well-nigh impossible to establish beyond doubt what really happened, for all those involved had too much to lose or gain by being completely honest. Getting to the bottom of such mysteries can be a fascinating piece of detective work but is perhaps less important than trying to understand how contemporaries perceived the events in question and how they reacted to them.

It is not only contemporaries who filter events to fit preconceptions. Historians passing judgement on 1917 have not been free from bias and have reached radically differing conclusions. Some historians, including modern Soviet ones, argue that the October Revolution was historically inevitable and the Provisional Government bound to fail. Others argue that Bolshevik success depended on a chance constellation of favourable circumstances that might never have been repeated if the first opportunity had been missed. The role of the individual as a shaper of history has also been debated at length, particularly in regard to Lenin. Was he merely swept along by forces beyond his control, or was he a shrewd politician who grasped the unique opportunity that the chaos of 1917 offered to anyone unscrupulous enough to seize it? Were Lenin's opponents *destined* to be swept into the "dustbin of history" (in Trotsky's memorable phrase), or did they bring their fate on themselves by pursuing mistaken policies that could have been altered by act of will?

There is nothing mysterious about the craft of an historian. The most important tools are an alert mind, common sense and a dash of healthy scepticism, which accepts nothing at face value until it has been thoroughly evaluated. Neither is the study of even the most distant past less important to our lives than the study of more obviously "relevant" subjects. From it we may become aware that our own judgements about events happening now may likewise be the products of inherited prejudices, and that the "truth" presented by the media and those in authority over us may be equally subject to bias. If we realize this, we have taken a step on the road to making more informed and rational judgements about the issues of our own time.

Ten Days that Shook the World

"Ten Days that Shook the World" is the title of a book by John Reed (see page 61).

By the beginning of November 1917 Russian politics were in turmoil. The Provisional Government, which had ruled the country since March and which was supported by the middle classes and by the majority of moderate socialists of the Menshevik and Socialist Revolutionary parties, was being challenged by the Bolsheviks, a radical socialist party led by Lenin and Trotsky. Whether or not the Government could withstand a Bolshevik insurrection would depend on the amount of support it could count on from the ordinary Russian people, especially in the capital, Petrograd, and in the other large cities. Of crucial and immediate importance would be the attitudes of the factory workers and of the soldiers and sailors who garrisoned Petrograd and the neighbouring naval base of Kronstadt.

The majority of Russian soldiers, though, were not in the cities but strung out in a thousand-mile front along Russia's western border, where they had been fighting the Germans since 1914. If Petrograd fell to the Bolsheviks, it might still be possible for the Government to retake the city by calling up loyal troops from the front.

The Provisional Government was aware of its vulnerability. In its public statements it stressed that the elections for the Constituent Assembly, scheduled for the end of November, would give the Russian people their first-ever opportunity to express their democratic will and establish a government representing *all* Russians. It would be foolish, therefore, to allow an armed minority, representing only a fraction of the population, to seize power. The Bolsheviks did not agree, arguing that they represented the true will of the mass of ordinary people.

DAY ONE: 6 NOVEMBER 1917

Orders issued to the Petrograd Garrison by Colonel Polkovnikov, Commander of the Petrograd Military District:

1. I order all units to remain in the barracks where they are stationed until orders are received from the staff of the district. I forbid any independent demonstrations. All who demonstrate with arms on the streets contrary to this order will be tried for armed rebellion . . .
3. I categorically forbid the troops to carry out any "orders" emanating from various organizations.

Resolution by the Petrograd Garrison:

The time for words is past. The country is on the verge of ruin. The army demands peace, the peasants land and the workers bread and work. The Coalition [Provisional] Government is against the people. It has become the tool of the enemies of the people. . . . The All-Russian Congress of Soviets must take power into its own hands in order to give to the people peace, bread and land. Only thus can the safety of the revolution be assured.

Telegram from Colonel Polkovnikov to General Dukhonin, Commander-in-Chief at the Front:

I report that the situation in Petrograd is threatening. There are no street outbreaks or disorders, but a systematic seizure of institutions and stations is going on. No orders are carried out. The junkers [military cadets] give up their posts without resistance. The Cossacks, notwithstanding a number of orders, have not come out of their barracks up to this time. Recognizing all my responsibility before the country, I report that the Provisional Government is in danger of losing all its power, and there are no guarantees that there will not be attempts to seize the Government.

**DAY TWO:
7 NOVEMBER 1917**

During the night of 6-7 November, the Red Guard, the Bolshevik private army of factory workers, Kronstadt sailors and garrison soldiers, occupied the printing presses of non-Communist newspapers, the telephone exchange, post office and main bridges across the River Neva. The crew of the cruiser, *Aurora*, ordered by the Provisional Government to defend the Winter Palace, defected and trained their guns on the palace itself, where the ministers were sheltering.

Petrograd, 1917.

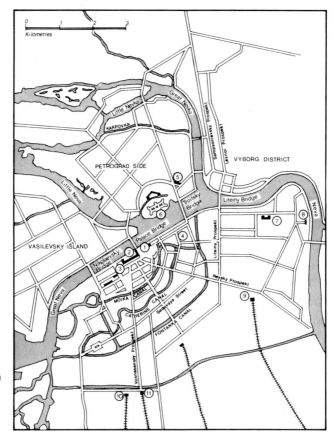

1 Winter Palace
2 Admiralty
3 Mikhailovsky Riding
   School
4 Field of Mars
5 Ksheshinskaya Palace
6 Peter and Paul Fortress
7 Tauride Palace
   (headquarters of the
   Soviet)
8 Smolny Institute
   (Bolshevik headquarters)
9 Nikolaevsky (Moscow)
   Station
10 Baltic Station
11 Warsaw Station

These events coincided with the opening session of the 2nd All-Russian Congress of Soviets, a conference of socialists sent by local soviets from all over the country. Before this assembly of their peers, Lenin and Trotsky defended their actions against two serious criticisms. Firstly, argued the Mensheviks and Socialist Revolutionaries, the Bolsheviks did not represent all the ordinary Russian people. Only a broadly-based coalition of all socialist parties could do that. Secondly, the argument continued, the Bolshevik revolution was premature. Most of the Bolsheviks' support came from Russians who were disgruntled with the present system but who had no real grasp of what Bolshevism stood for. In those circumstances it was unlikely that the Bolsheviks would be able to retain power for long, and the resulting backlash would set back the cause of socialism for decades.

So, there were two separate struggles taking place in the second week of November 1917. At noisy meetings, in smoke-filled halls, the Bolsheviks and their opponents debated the wisdom and long-term implications of the coup. Meanwhile the real battle for the fate of the revolution was taking place on the streets of the capital, where adherents of the Provisional Government vied with the Bolsheviks for the hearts and minds of the masses. The picture was all the more confusing because the two struggles influenced each other. As news from the streets filtered into the Soviet, so the debate shifted to take account of new circumstances.

It is unfortunate for posterity that many of the really crucial moments went unrecorded, whereas verbatim accounts of politicians' speeches are usually readily available. Only when an enterprising reporter like the American, John Reed, went on to the streets do we catch a glimpse of the emotions and arguments that swayed the ordinary Russians.

Power struggles are rarely simple, two-sided affairs. In November 1917 Russian opinion ranged itself along all points of a spectrum from outright opposition to the Bolsheviks to enthusiastic support for them, and it may be that the failure of key groups to act decisively on one side or the other was one of the most important factors in deciding the outcome.

Bolshevik Pamphlet distributed to the Cossacks defending the Winter Palace:

You, Cossacks, are being incited against us workers and soldiers. This plan of Cain is being put into operation by our common enemies, the oppressors, the privileged classes – generals, bankers, landlords, former officials, former servants of the Tsar. . . . They are ready at any moment to destroy the Petrograd Soviet and crush the Revolution.

On the evening of 7 November the Winter Palace fell with hardly a shot being fired and the captured ministers were imprisoned in the Peter and Paul fortress. Prime Minister Kerensky, however, escaped and fled to the front to raise troops. Just before midnight, Schreider, the mayor of Petrograd, and Prokopopitch, Minister of Supply in the Provisional Government, who had not been captured with the others, led a march to the Winter Palace to protest against Bolshevik activities. However, the demonstrators were soon dispersed by a detachment of armed sailors.

Къ Гражданамъ Россіи.

Временное Правительство низложено. Государственная власть перешла въ руки органа Петроградскаго Совѣта Рабочихъ и Солдатскихъ Депутатовъ Военно-Революціоннаго Комитета, стоящаго во главѣ Петроградскаго пролетаріата и гарнизона.

Дѣло, за которое боролся народъ: немедленное предложеніе демократическаго мира, отмѣна помѣщичьей собственности на землю, рабочій контроль надъ производствомъ, созданіе Совѣтскаго Правительства — это дѣло обезпечено.

ДА ЗДРАВСТВУЕТЪ РЕВОЛЮЦІЯ РАБОЧИХЪ, СОЛДАТЪ И КРЕСТЬЯНЫ

Военно-Революціонный Комитетъ
при Петроградскомъ Совѣтѣ
Рабочихъ и Солдатскихъ Депутатовъ.

25 октября 1917 г. 10 ч. утра.

◁ Proclamation issued by the Military Revolutionary Committee to the Citizens of Russia, 7 November 1917.
Translation:
To the citizens of Russia! The Provisional Government is deposed. The State power has passed into the hands of the organ of the Petrograd Soviet of Workers' and Soldiers' Deputies, the Military Revolutionary Committee, which stands at the head of the Petrograd proletariat and garrison.
The cause for which the people were fighting: immediate proposal of a democratic peace, abolition of landlord property rights over the land, labour control of production, creation of a soviet government – that cause is securely achieved.
LONG LIVE THE REVOLUTION OF WORKMEN, SOLDIERS AND PEASANTS!
Military Revolutionary Committee
Petrograd Soviet of Workers' and Soldiers' Deputies
25 October

A cartoon from Pravda,▷ *8 November. Middle-class demonstrators against the "illegal" Bolshevik seizure of power are kindly but sternly dismissed by a young sailor, a representative of the will of the common people.*

At 10.45 pm the opening session of the All-Russian Congress of Soviets convened.

Trotsky's Speech to the Congress:

A rising of the masses of the people needs no justification. What has happened is an insurrection, and not a conspiracy. We hardened the revolutionary energy of the Petersburg workers and soldiers. . . . The masses of the people followed our banner and our insurrection was victorious. And now we are told: renounce your victory, make concessions, compromise. With whom? I ask: with whom ought we to compromise . . . to those who tell us to do this we must say: you are miserable bankrupts, your role is played out; go where you ought to be: into the dustbin of history!

Lieber's (Menshevik) Reply to Trotsky:

Engels and Marx said that the proletariat had no right to take power until it was ready for it. In a bourgeois revolution like this . . . the seizure of power by the masses means the tragic end of the Revolution.

A Soldier's Speech to the Congress:

Comrades . . . I speak for the 2nd Lettish Rifles. You have heard the statements of the two representatives of the Army Committees [opposing the Bolshevik seizure of power]; these statements would have had some value if their authors had been representative of the army. But they do not represent the soldiers. . . . I tell you, the Lettish soldiers have many times said, "No more resolutions! No more talk! We want deeds – the Power must be in our hands!"

Before midnight on 7 November Kerensky arrived at Pskov, headquarters of the north-west front. His mission was to raise an army loyal to the Provisional Government and to wrest back control of Petrograd from the Bolsheviks.

DAY THREE: 8 NOVEMBER 1917

The first of the troops dispatched by Kerensky from the front arrived in the capital at dawn. They were the Third Cycle Battalion. Their spokesman reported:

A joint meeting was held among the cyclists and not a single man was found willing to shed the blood of his fathers, or to support a government of bourgeois and landowners.

A Manifesto written by the Socialist Revolutionary Party and which was pinned up on walls and fences throughout Petrograd:

1. The seizure of power carried out by the Bolshevik Party and by the Petrograd Soviet of Workers' and Soldiers' Deputies on the eve of the Constituent Assembly . . . is a crime against the motherland and the Revolution, signalizes the beginning of civil war and the breakup of the Constituent Assembly and threatens to destroy the Revolution.
2. In anticipation of the outbreak of popular indignation, which is inevitable as a result of the unavoidable breakdown of Bolshevik promises, which are obviously unobtainable at the present time, the Socialist Revolutionary faction summons all the revolutionary forces of the country to organize and stand on guard for the Revolution, in order, in the event of an impending catastrophe, to be able to take the fate of the country into their own hands.

That night another session of the All-Russian Soviet Congress opened. Before this assembly, the Bolsheviks announced that they were now the official government of Russia, adopted the name "Government of People's Commissars" and outlined their new policies: 1. A proclamation to the peoples of all the fighting nations, proposing an immediate peace without annexations and indemnities; and 2. A decree ordering the confiscation without compensation of all privately-owned land and its transference to those who tilled it.

Avilov's Speech to the Congress: a Menshevik View:

We must ask ourselves where we are going. . . . The ease with which the coalition government was upset cannot be explained by the strength of the left-wing, but by the incapacity of the government to give the people peace and bread. And the left-wing cannot maintain itself in power unless it can solve these questions . . .

Can it give bread to the people? Grain is scarce. The majority of peasants will not be with you, for you cannot give them the machinery they need. Fuel and other primary necessities are almost impossible to procure . . .

As for peace, that will be even more difficult. . . . They [the Allies] will never accept the proposition of a peace conference from *you*. You will not be recognized either in London and Paris or in Berlin . . .

You cannot count on the effective help of the proletariat of the Allied countries because in most countries it is very far from the revolutionary struggle. . . . The isolation of Russia will fatally result either in the defeat of the Russian army by the Germans, and the patching up of a peace between the Austro-German coalition and the Franco-British coalition *at the expense of Russia*, or in a separate peace with Germany.

Trotsky's Reply:

These considerations on the danger of the isolation of our party are not new. On the eve of insurrection our fatal defeat was also predicted. Everybody was against us. . . . How is it that we were able to overturn the government almost without bloodshed? That fact is the most striking proof that we were not isolated. In reality the Provisional Government was isolated; the democratic parties which march against us are isolated, and forever cut off from the proletariat.

News from outside Petrograd:
The Moscow garrison had voted 116-18 in favour of supporting a Bolshevik uprising in the city. The Rada, Ukrainian nationalists, had taken over Kiev. The Mensheviks had seized power in Tbilisi in Georgia. (They were eventually to declare Georgia an independent republic.)

DAY FOUR:
9 NOVEMBER 1917

A Telegram sent to Petrograd by Ataman Kaledin of the Don Cossacks:

Novocherkassk, 8 November
In view of the revolt of the Bolsheviki, and their attempt to depose the Provisional Government and to seize power in Petrograd. . . . The Cossack Government declares that it considers the acts criminal and

absolutely inadmissable. . . . Until the return of the Provisional Government to power and the restoration of order in Russia, I have taken upon myself, beginning 7 November, all power in that which concerns the region of the Don.

Kerensky meanwhile was continuing his efforts to raise an army. General Krasnov undertook to mobilize troops on the north-western front for an assault on Petrograd in the name of the Provisional Government. The Bolsheviks launched a propaganda campaign to convince both the people of the capital and Krasnov's soldiers that Kerensky was their enemy.

At the Grenadier barracks in Petrograd, the regiment discusses where its allegiance lies. The decision of most of the city garrisons not to oppose the Bolshevik coup may have been the most crucial factor in deciding the fate of the October Revolution.

General Krasnov appeals to Troops at the North-West Front:

Citizen soldiers . . . all you who have remained true to your soldier's oath . . . to you I turn with an appeal to go and save Petrograd from anarchy, violence and hunger, and Russia from the indelible mark of shame which has been thrown on it by a dark handful of ignorant men, led by the will and money of Emperor Wilhelm.

The Provisional Government, to which you pledged allegiance in the great days of March, is not overthrown, but has been violently driven from its headquarters and holds its sessions with the great army at the front.

Article in *Pravda*:

What is Kerensky?
A usurper, whose place is in the Peter and Paul prison, with Kornilov and Kishkin.
A criminal, a traitor to the workers, soldiers and peasants, who believed in him.

Kerensky? A murderer of soldiers!
Kerensky? A public executioner of peasants!
Kerensky? A strangler of workers!
Such is the second Kornilov who now wants to butcher liberty.

As news of Krasnov's advance reached Petrograd, some regiments of the garrison wavered in their support for the Bolsheviks and planned to stay neutral in the coming battle. At the Mikhailovsky Riding School, headquarters of a leading armoured car troop, a debate took place:

Lieutenant Kranjunov:

It is an awful thing for Russians to kill their Russian brothers. There must not be civil war between soldiers who stood shoulder to shoulder against the Tsar and conquered the foreign enemy in battles which will go down in history! What have we soldiers got to do with the squabbles of political parties!

Krylenko, a Bolshevik:

I don't need to tell you that I am a soldier.
I don't need to tell you that I want peace.
What I must say is that the Bolshevik Party, successful in the Workers' and Soldiers' Revolution by the help of you and all the rest of the brave comrades who have hurled down for ever the power of the bloodthirsty bourgeoisie, promised to offer peace to all the peoples, and that has already been done – today!

You were asked to remain neutral – to remain neutral while the junkers and the Death Battalions, who are never neutral, shoot us down in the streets and bring back to Petrograd Kerensky – or perhaps some other of the old gang . . .

The government is in your hands. You are the masters. Great Russia belongs to you. Will you give it back?

DAY FIVE:
10 NOVEMBER 1917

Krasnov's mainly Cossack troops reached Gatchina, twenty miles from Petrograd, and were quartered in the museum there. Count Zubov, the curator, overheard a conversation in which a Cossack remarked: "What have we to do with Russia, Kerensky and the Bolsheviks? Let's go to the Don. The Bolsheviks will not go there."

In Moscow the Kremlin, hitherto held by pro-Bolshevik troops, had surrendered to the forces of the Provisional Government. In Saratov, on the Volga, local Bolsheviks had seized power but the city was threatened by a battalion of Cossacks.

DAY SIX:
11 NOVEMBER 1917

Bolshevik Poster appealing to the People of Petrograd:

Citizens of Petrograd! Kerensky fled from the city . . . abandoning you to the Germans, to famine, to bloody massacres. The revolting people have arrested Kerensky's ministers and you have seen how the ordering and supplying of Petrograd at once improved. Kerensky, at the demand of the aristocrat proprietors, the capitalists, speculators, marches against you for the purpose of giving back the land to the landowners and continuing the hated and ruinous war.

Citizens of Petrograd! We know that the great majority of you are in favour of the people's revolutionary authority. Do not be deceived by the lying declaration of the bourgeois conspirators, who will be ruthlessly crushed.

Workers, soldiers and peasants! We call upon you for revolutionary devotion and discipline.

Millions of peasants and soldiers are with us.

DAY SEVEN: 12 NOVEMBER 1917

In Moscow the battle had reached stalemate and a truce had been arranged between the Red Guard and the troops supporting the Provisional Government.

In Petrograd, however, the military situation had come to a climax. During the night of 11-12 November a makeshift army of pro-Bolshevik workers, soldiers and sailors had defeated Krasnov's demoralized troops in the Petrograd suburb of Pulkovo. When the news reached the capital, the Bolsheviks were elated. A message from Trotsky, who was with the army at Pulkovo, was read to the Soviet Congress at 2 am:

The night of 30 to 31 October [11-12 November] will go down in history. The attempt of Kerensky to move counter-revolutionary troops against the capital of the Revolution has been decisively repulsed. Kerensky is retreating; we are advancing. The soldiers, sailors and workers of Petrograd have shown that they can and will with arms in their hands enforce the will and authority of democracy . . .

The grand idea of the domination of the worker and peasant democracy closed the ranks of the army and stiffened its will. All the country from now on will be convinced that the power of the Soviets is no ephemeral thing but an invincible fact. . . . The repulse of Kerensky is the confirmation of the right of the people to a peaceful, free life, to land, to bread, to power.

The debate over the morality of the Bolshevik coup rumbled on.

Speech by Pinkevitch, a Menshevik, to the City Councillors at the Petrograd City Duma [town hall]:

If everything that is against the Bolsheviki is counter-revolutionary, then I do not know the difference between revolution and anarchy. . . . The Bolsheviki are depending upon the passions of the unbridled masses; we have nothing but moral force.

DAY EIGHT: 13 NOVEMBER 1917

Sailors from the battleships stationed in Sevastopol had forced their officers to take an oath of allegiance to the Bolshevik government. Street fighting was taking place in Kazan, between pro-Provisional Government artillery and the local Bolsheviks. The telephone exchange in Moscow had been captured by the Red Guard.

DAY NINE:
14 NOVEMBER 1917
In Petrograd the Bolsheviks were still nervous. Although the Cossacks had been defeated at the Battle of Pulkovo, their continued presence near the capital constituted a danger to the new regime.

Appeal by Dibenko, a Bolshevik, to the Cossacks near Pulkovo:

The government appeals to the troops which march under the flag of counter-revolution, and invites them immediately to lay down their arms – to shed no longer the blood of their brothers in the interests of a handful of landowners and capitalists. The Workers', Soldiers' and Peasants' Revolution curses those who remain even for a moment under the flag of the People's enemies . . .

Cossacks! Come over to the rank of the victorious people! Railwaymen, postmen, telegraphers – all, all support the new Government of the People!

The cities and provinces of European Russia.

The Cossacks disbanded. One of their officers explained to John Reed that they were tired of being used by governments to put down revolutions. They had nothing against the Bolsheviks, who promised that "they will not take away our land. There is no danger to us. We remain neutral."

DAY TEN:
15 NOVEMBER 1917

In Moscow the Provisional Government's forces had surrendered and the Bolsheviks were in complete control of the city. A Bolshevik regime had been firmly established in Baku, centre of Russia's oil industry.

Editorial in *Novaya Zhizn*, one of the few non-Bolshevik papers still published:

From day to day the Government of People's Commissars sinks deeper and deeper into the mire of superficial haste. Having easily conquered power . . . the Bolsheviks cannot make use of it.

Powerless to direct the existing mechanism of government, they are unable at the same time to create a new one which might work easily and freely according to the theories of the social experimenters.

Just a little while ago the Bolsheviks hadn't enough men to run their growing party – a work above all of speakers and writers; where then are they going to find trained men to execute the diverse and complicated functions of government?

The new government acts and threatens, it sprays the country with decrees, each one more radical and more "socialist" than the last. But in this exhibition of socialism on paper – more likely designed for the stupefaction of our descendants – there appears neither the desire nor the capacity to solve the immediate problems of the day.

Lenin's Reply in *Pravda*:

Shame upon those who are of little faith, who doubt, who allow themselves to be frightened by the bourgeoisie. . . . There is NOT A SHADOW of hesitation in the masses of Petrograd, Moscow and the rest of Russia.

We shall not submit to any ultimatum from small groups of intellectuals which are not followed by the masses.

THINGS TO DO AND THINK ABOUT:

Relatively little blood was shed during the Petrograd coup, primarily because Provisional Government forces put up such feeble resistance. How many individuals and groups can you find who are actively on the side of the Government? There are not many – the ministers themselves, civil servants, Menshevik and Socialist Revolutionary politicians, army officers like Polkovnikov and Krasnov. You might assume that if such authority figures were backing the Government, many others would automatically follow. In fact, this did not happen in November 1917, especially among the garrison troops and the soldiers at the front. Can you identify the crucial points at which troops failed to respond to the pleas of the Government?

Not everywhere did the transfer of power proceed as smoothly as in Petrograd. Nine days of sporadic but bloody fighting left these barricades on Moscow's Krasnaya Presnya.

Some military units were decidedly pro-Bolshevik; others were just indifferent to the outgoing Government's fate and let the Bolsheviks in by default. Can you distinguish which were which? Later sections of this book should throw some light on how the Bolsheviks were able to lure the soldiers from their allegiance.

The Bolsheviks were elated by their success but the moderate socialists were horrified. Do the extracts in this section give you any clues about the reasons for their disapproval?

Concentrating on Petrograd can give a misleading picture. Russia is a vast country and Bolshevik rule would not be secure until effective control had been established over all the large centres of population. Very few cities fell as quickly or as easily as Petrograd. In some – can you name them? – the struggle was bloodier and more prolonged. In other areas a period of chaos resulted in the establishment of non-Bolshevik regimes. The reasons for this patchwork result are beyond the scope of this book, but the following factors sometimes played a part:
- distance from Petrograd and Moscow
- a strong sense of local identity, especially among the non-Russian nationalities
- a low level of industrialization, for Bolshevism was first and foremost an urban phenomenon.

On the map of Russia on page 14 locate those cities where the Bolsheviks managed to secure power in November 1917 and those where they did not.

Filling in the Background:
An Economy Under Stress

The two and a half decades between 1890 and 1914 were years of rapid industrial expansion and urbanization, aimed at converting backward agrarian Russia into a modern industrial power.

Increase in Factory Production, 1887-1908:

YEAR	NUMBER OF WORKERS	TOTAL PRODUCTION (in millions of roubles)
1887	1,318,000	1334.5
1897	2,098,000	2839.1
1908	2,609,000	4909.0

Expansion of Russia's Major Cities:

	NUMBER OF INHABITANTS (in thousands)	
	1897	1914
Moscow	1038.6	1762.7
St Petersburg (Petrograd)	1264.9	2118.5
Kiev	257.7	520.5
Baku	111.9	232.2
Tashkent	155.7	271.9
Tiflis (Tbilisi)	159.6	307.3

Production of Major Commodities:

	(in millions of poods)	
	1900	1913
Pig iron	177	283
Steel	163	246
Steel rails	30.2	35.6
Coal	1003.0	2214.0
Copper	0.5	2.0

(*Source:* G. Katkov (Ed.), *Russia Enters the Twentieth Century*, London, 1971)

Figures, however, do not tell us the full story. On their own, these cannot tell how Russia's industrial capacity compared with that of her European neighbours, a factor of some importance when we come to evaluate Russia's performance in the First World War. Nor do the figures reveal the sort of social and political stresses that might be engendered by so rapid a pace of industrialization. There are two major points to keep in mind. Firstly, industrialization in Tsarist Russia was not the result of the activities of an enterprising middle class, as had been the case in most of Western Europe and the United States. It was initiated and financed by a government anxious to catch up with the rest of the developed world. The Russian commercial middle class or bourgeoisie remained, therefore, comparatively weak, and this may help to explain why middle-class agitation for the development of parliamentary government was easily crushed before, during and after 1917. Secondly, there was a danger that the speed at which factories were built after 1890 would outstrip the provision made for the men who worked in them. The following table, listing rates of compensation for industrial accidents, which was pinned up in the workshops of the Obukhov munitions factory in Petrograd in the years before 1914, indicates that some employers, at least, placed a low value on the health and safety of the industrial worker.

Rates of Compensation

		Right hand	Left hand
HEAD	1. Cerebral lesion, causing serious difficulties		100 roubles
	2. Cerebral lesion, uncovering the flesh but without serious consequences		70 roubles
	3. Lighter cerebral wound		30 roubles
	4. Cerebral contusion		60-85 roubles
EYES	1. Loss of sight in both eyes		100 roubles
	2. Loss of sight in one eye		35 roubles
EARS	1. Deafness in both ears		50 roubles
	2. Deafness in one ear		10 roubles
FACE	1. Loss of speech		40 roubles
	2. Damage to face, harmful to the working senses		35 roubles
BACK	1. Broken vertebral column		100 roubles
	2. Damage generally to the back		10-50 roubles
LIMBS		Right hand	Left hand
	1. Loss of a thumb	30 roubles	25 roubles
	2. Loss of index finger	25 roubles	15 roubles
	3. Loss of 3rd or 4th finger	10 roubles	5 roubles
	4. Loss of little finger	5 roubles	–
	5. Loss of all fingers	75 roubles	65 roubles
	6. Loss of hand	75 roubles	65 roubles
	7. Loss of both hands	100 roubles	

The average monthly wage in Moscow in 1914 was 22 roubles.

(*Source:* M. Ferro, *October 1917. A Social History of the Russian Revolution, London, 1980*)

A clear indication that rapid industrialization might cause political strains was given in 1905. In January of that year a huge demonstration of Petrograd workers attempted to present a petition to the Tsar asking for improved wages and working conditions. When the demonstrators were forcibly dispersed by armed troops and hundreds were killed in the ensuing panic, the capital erupted. By October a general strike had brought Russian industry and commerce almost to a standstill.

CONDITIONS IN THE COUNTRYSIDE

As late as 1914 four-fifths of the Russian population were peasants. In 1861 the archaic institution of serfdom had been abolished and the "liberated" peasant had been granted an allotment of land carved from his former

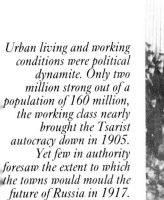

Urban living and working conditions were political dynamite. Only two million strong out of a population of 160 million, the working class nearly brought the Tsarist autocracy down in 1905. Yet few in authority foresaw the extent to which the towns would mould the future of Russia in 1917.

master's estate. These allotments, however, were sometimes less than the area the peasant had farmed before emancipation.

Percentage Reduction in Peasant Holdings in Selected Areas, after 1861 Emancipation Settlement:

Poltava	37.2	Samara	41.8
Kharkov	28.3	Saratov	37.9
Tambov	20.6	Ekaterinoslav	37.6
Kursk	18.9	Simbirsk	27.8

(*Source:* G. Katkov, *Russia Enters the Twentieth Century*, London, 1971)

Moreover, land was not granted to the peasants outright. Landlords were given compensation by the Government for lands given up, and the peasants were expected to repay the state in installments over a period of 49 years. By 1900 accumulated arrears meant that these "redemption payments" would not be completed until the 1950s.

In common with much of the rest of Europe, late nineteenth-century rural Russia experienced a population explosion. Peasant holdings frequently had to be sub-divided to provide for ever larger numbers of children, and more and more farmers found themselves with a plot which was barely big enough to support a family in a good year. Crop failures and famines were frequent, and the poor harvests of 1901 and 1904 were followed by serious unrest, particularly in 1905-6. Among the provinces most seriously affected were Poltava, Kharkov, Saratov, Tambov and Kursk, areas that figure in the table above. Think about what connections there might be between the statistics and the actual events of 1905.

1905 – THE CONTEMPORARY DEBATE

The events of 1905-6 forced the Tsarist Government to think seriously about rural problems for the first time in years. Admiral Dubasov, who led military expeditions to suppress the riots in Kursk Province, reported to the Tsar that the peasants there attributed all their hardships to a shortage of land and had decided to burn out the landlords and seize it for themselves. The authorities, however, reacted in different ways.

> I am a country gentleman myself, and I shall be very glad to give up half my land for nothing, in the conviction that only thus can I keep the other half for myself.

(Count D.F. Trepov, Palace Commandant to Tsar Nicholas II, 1905)

> Private property must remain sacrosanct.

(The Tsar, 1905)

> The Russian peasant has a passionate desire to level everyone, to bring everyone to one standard of living; and because it is impossible to raise the mass to the level of the most active and clever, the best elements must be brought down to that of the inferior inert majority. Individual property ownership is the best antidote to communal ownership. It is the guarantee of order, because the small proprietor is the basis on which stable conditions in the state can rest.

(P. Stolypin, Governor of Saratov Province, 1905)

You may find the last argument rather difficult to understand. What Stolypin proposed was to provide the credit and the legal framework to encourage the more prosperous peasant to buy out his less successful neighbours, and thus to create an elite class of comfortably-off peasant farmers – *Kulaks* – who would repay the state with loyalty. The scheme did not envisage releasing any more land from private estates into the pool available to peasants. It had the added advantage, from the Government's point of view, of creating a landless class who would tend to drift to the new industrial towns.

This was the "solution" to peasant unrest that was officially adopted between 1907 and 1914. It is generally estimated that between 10 and 15 per cent of peasant households obtained more or better land as a result and thus achieved a significant improvement in their standard of living. Many more enjoyed no benefits or were squeezed off the land altogether. However, Stolypin's reforms were abruptly terminated by the outbreak of war in 1914 and no one can tell what would have happened had the scheme continued for another decade or so.

THINGS TO DO AND THINK ABOUT:

Judging by the amount of pen and ink expended on the respective problems, the authorities seem to have been far more worried by rural than by urban discontent. Although the working class were but a fraction of the population, the Tsar and his government may have been making a serious misjudgement here. The events of 1905 demonstrated that urban workers may wield a political influence out of all proportion to their numbers. Can you work out why this should be? Bear this in mind as you study the rest of this book.

Filling in the Background:
The War, 1914-17

How the Russian Empire might have developed had war not intervened is still a subject of debate. The one thing that historians do agree on is that the prolonged conflict on the Eastern Front between 1914 and 1917 made some sort of upheaval in Russia inevitable.

A SELF-PERPETUATING WAR

For the Tsarist Empire, involvement in the Great War began on 28 August 1914, when Austria-Hungary declared war on Russia's ally, Serbia. Within seven days the European continent was effectively divided into two warring camps: the Allies, Britain, France, Russia, Belgium and Serbia (later joined by Italy and the United States) versus the Central Powers, Germany and Austria-Hungary (later joined by Turkey and Bulgaria).

The opening months of the war resulted in such carnage that none of the protagonists would dream of withdrawing until they had made gains that would "justify" their losses. Britain and France refused to consider peace until Germany had been utterly crushed, and the Tsar, sincerely eager to prove a dependable ally, went along with this. Moreover, once Turkey had joined the Central Powers, the Russian Government was reluctant to stop fighting until the ancient Russian ambition of annexing Constantinople, the Turkish capital, had been fulfilled. The Great War had become self-perpetuating.

Most of the fighting in Europe took place on two main fronts. While the British, French and Germans fought four years of trench warfare in the West, a more fluid war developed on the Eastern Front, where the frontiers of the Russian Empire met Germany and Austria-Hungary. A Russian invasion of German East Prussia in August 1914 was repulsed at the battles of Tannenberg and the Masurian Lakes, with 225,000 Russian prisoners being taken. Between May and July 1915 the Central Powers occupied the Kingdom of Warsaw (now in Poland), Lithuania and Western Latvia, all of which had been part of the Russian Empire since the eighteenth century, Such huge territorial losses made the Tsarist Government even more reluctant to bring an early end to the fighting.

In June 1916 the Russian army launched an offensive — named the "Brusilov Offensive", after its commander — against the Austrian armies on the southern part of the front. It succeeded brilliantly until the Germans moved troops to the aid of their ally. Rapidly, the Russian armies were halted and forced to move back to where they had started from. Over a million Russian soldiers were killed, captured or seriously wounded.

Altogether, Russian losses in the two and a half years of war between August 1914 and March 1917 were staggering:

Killed	1,300,000
Wounded	4,200,000
Prisoners	2,500,000
Total losses	8,000,000

In order to understand the reasons for military failure and the effect it had on domestic politics, we must now return to the point made on page 17 that Russia's impressive industrialization figures cannot be accepted at face value. Here is a comparison of heavy industrial production in Tsarist Russia and other major powers:

Mineral Production, 1912:

	Millions of £s sterling
USA	392
Great Britain	123
Germany	104
Russia	83
France	29
Austria-Hungary	22

Production of Pig Iron, 1913:

	Thousands of tons
USA	31,426
Germany	19,312
Great Britain	10,455
France	5,311
Russia	4,635
Austria-Hungary	2,435

Production of Steel, 1913:

	Thousands of tons
USA	31,803
Germany	18,329
Great Britain	7,787
Russia	4,841
France	4,687
Austria-Hungary	2,683

(*Source:* G. Katkov (Ed.), *Russia Enters the Twentieth Century,* London, 1921)

In all these tables Russia comes no lower than fourth or fifth and in two of them has overtaken France. The really significant fact, however, is the size of the gap between Russia and her arch-enemy, Germany. Also, the number of men in the Russian army, all of whom had to be equipped and transported, was vastly greater than the number of men in the army of any other European power. What problems did the country suffer when it tried to fight a modern war on an inadequate industrial base?

THE ARMY Russian guns were sometimes limited to four shots a day or less and reinforcements often had to share rifles. Only 12% of the machine-guns needed were available on 1 January 1917 and throughout the war there was a serious shortage of barbed wire. The underdeveloped railway network was unable to cope with massive troop movements. Brusilov later wrote in his memoirs: "I knew that while we were entraining and transporting one army corps, the Germans could manage to transport three or four."

THE HOME FRONT Inadequate though the service might be, military requirements were given priority on the railways; the resultant shortage of transport for civilian purposes caused periodic bread shortages in the towns. With shortages came inflation and the real value of wages fell.

Average Wages for all Moscow Factories, 1914-16:

	Nominal	Real
	(in roubles)	
1914		
1st half	22.53	22.5
2nd half	21.18	20.8
1915		
1st half	23.35	19.5
2nd half	30.07	21.5
1916		
1st half	36.76	22.1
2nd half	46.42	19.5

(*Source:* M. Florinsky, *The End of the Russian Empire*, New York, 1961)

The slow progress towards a shorter working day was halted. During the war only 119,000 of Russia's three million industrial workers enjoyed an eight-hour day; 1,351,000 worked ten hours or more.

To this must be added the long-standing urban discontents we have already noticed. These did not disappear with the war but were exacerbated by it. As the number of workers in Petrograd, for example, grew from 234,000 (1910 census) to 400,000, any explosion of working-class discontent was liable to be even more dangerous to the stability of Tsarism than the upheavals of 1905 had been.

SUMMARY Whatever our opinion on the future development of Russia *without* the war, it seems unlikely that any government could have solved, in the short term, the horrendous problems that arose from waging total war in a semi-agrarian economy. Did the war then make revolution inevitable? The answer may have to be a tentative "probably", but political crisis may also have played a role. In the next chapter we shall see how the peoples and classes of Russia reacted to the deepening economic and human catastrophe of the Great War.

Filling in the Background: The Peoples of Russia

In 1914 the head of the Russian Government was Tsar Nicholas II, who enjoyed almost completely autocratic powers. The Council of Ministers, who helped the Tsar administer the country, could be appointed and dismissed by him, without reference to public opinion. The October Manifesto of 1905 had established a Duma or parliament, elected on a limited franchise, but its powers were very circumscribed (it did not, for example, have any control over the Tsar's choice of ministers) and it could

Live caricatures of Protopopov (left, Tsarist Minister of the Interior) and Rasputin are paraded through the streets of Petrograd after the February Revolution. The corruption and incompetence of his advisers tore away the last shreds of Nicholas II's prestige among all sections of the population, and by 1917 there were few who believed that the dynasty or the monarchy could survive.

be dissolved by the monarch at will. Nevertheless, it provided a barometer of middle-class opinion, as did the elected local councils known as *zemstvos*.

There were strict limits on all other forms of political activity. The press was censored and trade unions forbidden to take part in strikes or politics. In the first year of the war, middle-class voluntary organizations such as the All-Russian Union of Zemstvos had offered to assist the government by mobilizing the war industries in their areas, providing medical services for the army and so on. Fearing a dilution of the autocratic principle, the Tsar spurned the offer, and the Tsarist regime remained as autocratic and unresponsive to public opinion as ever.

How then did the social classes and political groups in Russia respond to the situation in which they found themselves between 1914 and 1917?

THE MIDDLE-CLASS VIEW

By 1914, two middle-class "liberal" political parties had been formed. The *Kadet* Party programme, drawn up in 1905, called for the establishment of a constitutional monarchy (in which the Tsar would rule in partnership with an elected parliament), the granting of full civil liberties to all Russian citizens and a moderate degree of land reform. The *Octobrists* were less radical. They were content with the limited powers granted to the Duma by the 1905 October Manifesto (hence the party name) and believed it could be used to pressurize the Tsar into governing more efficiently.

Middle-class attitudes towards the Tsarist Government and the war effort changed a great deal between 1914 and 1917.

Kadet Party Proclamation, 2 August 1914:

Whatever our attitude with regard to the government's domestic policies, it is our first duty to preserve our country, one and indivisible, and to maintain its position among the great powers. Let us lay aside our internal differences, and let us firmly keep in mind that in this hour our first and only task is to support our front fighters, with faith in the righteousness of our cause . . .

Motion passed by the Union of Zemstvos and Union of Towns, 27 September 1915:

In the tragic trials through which Russia is passing, we deem it our first duty to send a warm greeting to our stoical, glorious and dearly-loved army. The Russian people are more determined than ever to continue the war to victory, in loyal association with their faithful allies. But on the path to victory there lies a fatal obstacle created by all the vices of our political system, we mean irresponsible power, the absence of any link between the government and the country etc . . . in place of the present governors we must have men who enjoy the confidence of the nation.

Speech by P. Miliukov, Kadet Leader, in the Duma, 1 November 1916:

You must understand why we have no other task than to get rid of this government. You ask why we are carrying on this struggle in wartime. It is only in wartime that they are dangerous. They are dangerous to the war, and therefore in time of war, and in the name of the war, in the name of that which has united us, we shall fight them.

Something, however, always held the Kadets back from full-blooded opposition. An allegory was published in a Kadet newspaper in September 1915, which became known as the "Parable of the Mad Chauffeur". What would you do, the author asked, if you and your aged mother were speeding down a steep and precipitous road in a car driven by a chauffeur who was reckless, incompetent and perhaps insane? You could attempt to take over the car yourself by force but:

Can this be done on the steep mountain path? However skilful you are, however strong, the wheel is actually in his hands – he is steering the car, and one error in taking a turn, or an awkward movement of his hand, and the car is lost. You know that, and he knows it as well. And he mocks your anxiety and your helplessness: "You dare not touch me!"

He is right. You will not dare touch him. . . . So you will leave the steering-wheel in the hands of the chauffeur. Moreover, you will not try to hinder him – you will even help him with advice, warning, assistance. And you will be right, for this is what has to be done.

But how will you feel when you realize that your self-restraint might still be of no avail, and that even with your help the chauffeur will be unable to cope? How will you feel when your mother, having sensed the danger, begs you for help, and, misunderstanding your conduct, accuses you of inaction and indifference?

(*Source: Russkii Vedomosti* – "Russian Truth")

Can you work out what the author of the "Parable of the Mad Chauffeur" is really talking about? What are the Russian middle class so afraid of?

WORKING-CLASS VIEWS

The Leader of a Strike Movement at Stetnin Factory, Petrograd:

Comrades, my opinion is this. If we cannot get a loaf of bread for ourselves in a righteous way . . . we must go ahead and solve our problem by force. . . . Comrades, remember this also. Down with the Government! Down with the war! Comrades, arm yourselves with everything possible – bricks, rods, rocks, and go out of the factory and start smashing the first shops you find.

(*Source:* quoted in T. Hasegawa, *The February Revolution in Petrograd, 1917*, Seattle, 1981)

Strikes in Petrograd, August 1914 – February 1917:

MONTH	LOST WORKING DAYS
Aug. – Dec. 1914	4,787
Jan. – June 1915	16,657
July – Dec. 1915	402,329
Jan. – June 1916	1,124,878
July – Dec. 1916	634,295
Jan. – Feb. 1917	403,300

(*Source:* Hasegawa)

THE SOLDIERS' VIEW

A soldier had not only to contend with shortages of food and munitions at the front and a high probability of death or mutilation. He was also legally classified as a second-class citizen. He could not travel in a first- or second-class railway carriage nor eat in any restaurant except a third-class buffet. Civilians and officers were allowed to address him as "thou" instead of "you", a form of address otherwise used only for children and pets. Even when he was out of uniform, a soldier was expected to salute an officer if they passed on the street. Here are some extracts from soldiers' letters home, which were confiscated by the censor in 1916 and early 1917:

Persistent rumours have begun to circulate among the soldiers that peace will come soon. It's about time, as we're terribly sick and tired of the whole thing. (December)

They've put out an order that there will be no peace until full victory. And you know how badly they feed us – only beans for dinner and supper. Tell your comrades that we all ought to stage an uprising against the war. (January 1917)

There is no more bread, nothing to eat. We sit here for days on end without bread. Cold and hunger, nothing but deprivation. I'd rather be killed than starve like a dog. (February 1917)

In the trenches. In 1905 the Tsar survived because the army remained loyal; by 1917 widespread war-weariness had shattered the morale of the army and called its loyalty into serious question.

THE PEASANT VIEW

The Russian army was recruited from the peasantry and the views of the front line filtered through to the villages and vice versa. Moreover the land-hunger that had manifested itself so clearly before 1914 and was to surface again in 1917 did not disappear during the war years. To obtain a clear picture of how peasants felt about the land, the landlords, their wealthier neighbours (and by implication about Stolypin's reforms), study the following answers to a questionnaire sent by the Provisional Government to all villages just after the February Revolution.

Answers given by the Peasants of Ryazan:

1. Which procedure is more suitable in partition of the land; by individuals or by households?
Resolution: By household, among all inhabitants.
2. Are women to be excluded from distribution, or should land be partitioned among men and women alike?
Resolution: Distribution for all, without exception – men, women and children. . . .
4. How is it more just to distribute the land – should only peasants have some, or should any person prepared to work it?
Resolution: All inhabitants anxious to work it should have it . . .
7. Should land go to the workers with or without indemnity?
Resolution: No indemnity.
8. If without indemnity, who should pay the debts to the land banks?
Resolution: The government should find the means to pay them off.
9. What should be done in the case of those who bought their land in the last few years, often at very high prices?
Resolution: It should be seized without indemnity.
10. What is the most desirable form of soil utilization, by household or by commune?
Resolution: Household . . .
15. Once the working people have been given the land, all kinds of enterprises that supply seed, potato flour and bulls will disappear. How should these be acquired in the future?
Resolution: In every district there should be a kind of centre where the peasants can acquire what they need.

THINGS TO DO AND THINK ABOUT:

Is there much common ground between the masses and the middle classes? What are the issues that most divide them?

Although the middle classes toy with the idea of revolution, they fear that it will unleash forces that will prove impossible to control. Do you think there is any justification for this fear? If it comes to a clash for power between liberal politicians and the masses, who do you think is most likely to win? To a large extent, the story of 1917 is the story of this clash and its outcome.

Filling in the Background:
The Revolutionaries

Up to 1905 political parties and trade unions had been illegal in Russia (there were considerable restrictions on their activities after that date as well) and opponents of the Tsarist regime had been forced to use clandestine methods of operation. As prospects of a peaceful and gradual reform of the system seemed remote, it is hardly surprising that a number of revolutionary movements dedicated to a total and violent overthrow of the Tsarist state grew up. The revolutionary leaders came from the *intelligentsia*, those Russians, mainly from the middle and aristocratic classes, who had received a university education and whose studies had prompted them to think deeply about the shortcomings of their society and to search for possible solutions. You can find examples of such individuals in the biographies at the end of this book.

Out of this situation, however, grew a potential problem. Members by birth of a privileged elite, forced to spend long periods in prison or exile for their political convictions, the revolutionary intelligentsia had only limited contact with the common people in whose interests they claimed to act. There was always a danger that abstract theories, gleaned from books, might be dangerously out of touch with what the masses actually felt and wanted.

Middle-class intellectuals to a man! The Committee of the Petersburg League of Struggle for the Emancipation of the Working Class, 1897. Of the seven men pictured, only Lenin (seated in the middle) was to develop the ability to understand the moods and aspirations of the masses.

By 1917 there were three main revolutionary parties in Russia.

SOCIALIST REVOLUTION-ARIES   Founded in 1902, the Socialist Revolutionary Party had as its main belief that the violent overthrow of Tsarism must be followed by the nationalization of all land and its conversion from the personal property of individuals into a possession of the whole nation. Local authorities would then redistribute the land to individuals on the basis of "labour ownership" – i.e. only those who intended to cultivate the land themselves would be entitled to a share. The socialistically-minded peasants – so ran the argument of the delegates to the first Party Congress in 1905 – would then adopt a cooperative system of agriculture, thereby converting Russia in one step into a socialist state and by-passing the twin evils of capitalism and industrialization.

It is generally believed that the Socialist Revolutionary Party enjoyed widespread token support in the countryside before 1917, although in the absence of universal suffrage this is almost impossible to substantiate. All that can be offered by way of proof is to argue backwards from the Constituent Assembly elections of November 1917, when the party won over 50% of the votes. However, these figures may mislead, for it is likely that few peasants clearly understood for what they were actually casting their vote. A study of the answers given by the peasants of Ryazan (page 28) would indicate that it was individual, not communal ownership that they yearned for. Bear this in mind as you read the chapters that follow.

MENSHEVIKS The Mensheviks were one wing of the Russian Social Democratic Party, which had split into two factions in 1903. They followed faithfully the doctrines of Karl Marx, who argued that only when the revolution occurred in an advanced industrial nation with a numerous and politically-conscious working class (proletariat) would it result in *socialism* or *communism*, the perfect society in which the fruits of technology would be available to all, class distinctions disappear and working people run their own affairs without dictation from above. It was obvious to all Marxists, therefore, that backward Russia was far from ready for such a revolution and the overthrow of Tsarism would have to be followed by a lengthy period of pre-socialist government. This would take the shape of a middle-class or *bourgeois* democratic regime, during which time "worker pressure must dictate such conditions to them that the rule of the bourgeois democrats will from the outset bear within it the seeds of its own downfall" (Marx, 1849). Can you work out precisely what that quotation from Marx means?

It will not be obvious from what you have already read, but a further consequence followed from the Menshevik view of the correct road to socialism. If bourgeois democracy were an indispensable preliminary stage, it was essential that this did not collapse until it had fulfilled its historical usefulness. In the circumstances of 1917 this meant that Russia must be defended at all costs against conquest by Germany (the doctrine of "revolutionary defensism").

What, then, do you think Menshevik policy towards the war will be? Have you come across any other political group with the same views? What are the masses likely to think about it?

If the Tsar's departure is to be followed by an era of bourgeois democracy (whose duration cannot be specified but is likely to be measured in decades rather than years), which political party will the Mensheviks want to see inherit power? Are the proletariat and peasantry, few of whom are experts in Marxist theory, likely to accept this tamely, or will they expect something different to come out of the revolution? Bear these questions in mind as you study subsequent chapters.

BOLSHEVIKS The Bolsheviks were the other wing of the split Social Democratic Party. Inspired by Lenin, they planned to by-pass orthodox Marxist theory and proceed straight from Tsarist autocracy to a seizure of power by the peasants and proletariat. The political implications of this alteration in the Marxist order of historical progress were enormous. If a proletarian revolution became the priority, then it would be legitimate for revolutionaries to exploit ruthlessly any conditions that would hasten it along. For example, Bolsheviks should waste no time in defending Russian soil from a foreign enemy but instead concentrate on spreading through the Russian army "propaganda for the socialist revolution, for the necessity of turning their arms, not against their brothers, the hired slaves of other countries, but against the reactionary and bourgeois governments and parties of all countries" (Lenin, Vol. 5, 1914). Peasant land-hunger and urban food shortages might likewise be exploited in the interests of hastening the proletarian revolution. Even if the long-term aim of Bolshevism was a collectivized agriculture, Bolsheviks would be justified in pretending to be in favour of private ownership of land, in order to gain peasant backing for the seizure of power.

Lenin's opponents, before and since, have pointed out the dangers of this course. It might be possible to *seize* power through demagogy, but thereafter the masses might be required to make great sacrifices to ensure the survival of the revolution, sacrifices that they would not be politically mature enough to understand or accept. To survive, the Bolsheviks would be forced to establish a dictatorship.

Lenin saw things differently:

Since the revolution of 1905, Russia was governed by 130,000 landowners who did violence to 150 million people and imposed limitless repression on them . . . and now we are told that the . . . Bolshevik Party will not be able to lead and govern Russia, in the interests of the poor rather than the rich. . . . Besides we have a wonderful way of beginning our apparatus of state right away. . . . We will bring in the poorer classes to the daily toil of state management. . . . We are not Utopians, and we know that not just any cook or navvy will be able to run the state at once. What sets us apart from the Breshkovakayas, Tseretellis (Socialist Revolutionary and Menshevik) and the Kadets is that we demand an immediate breach with the prejudice according to which only rich functionaries of state, or civil servants from rich families, can administer that state and carry out the ordinary work of government.

(*Source:* Lenin, vol. 6)

You are not yet in a position to form your own opinion as to how justified the criticisms of Lenin are, but they are something else to bear in mind as you read this book.

March 1917: An Unplanned Revolution

By 1916 the Russian middle classes were disillusioned with the Tsarist Government because of its incompetent war effort. For the masses, however, the main problem was the war itself and the deleterious effect it was having on their already difficult lives. A mere transfer of power to the Kadets and Octobrists was unlikely to placate public opinion for long, especially as the breakdown in the transport system and the growing rumble of rural discontent were problems that could not be quickly or easily solved. In the wings waited the revolutionaries, although few of them clearly grasped the real mood of the Russian people.

In March 1917 the long-smouldering crisis came to a head. On the 8th of that month riots broke out in Petrograd among women queuing for food, and the movement spread quickly through the factories. Troops of the garrison, sent to quell the rioters, joined in and handed their weapons over to the demonstrators. As the news spread, similar riots occurred in other Russian cities.

A contemporary photograph of the streets of Petrograd on 10 March 1917, which was reproduced in an English magazine. Soldiers, including many Cossacks, have refused orders to fire on civilian demonstrators and have instead produced their own banners inscribed with the slogan, "Down with the monarchy".

EVENTS IN PETROGRAD, 8-12 MARCH

Leon Trotsky (a Bolshevik) looks back:

The fact is that the February Revolution was begun from below . . . the initiative being taken of their own accord by the most oppressed and downtrodden part of the proletariat – the women textile workers, among them no doubt many soldiers' wives. The overgrown breadlines had provided the last stimulus. About 90,000 workers, men and women, were on strike that day. The fighting mood expressed itself in demonstrations, meetings, encounters with the police . . . on the following day the movement not only fails to diminish but doubles. One half of the industrial workers of Petrograd are on strike on the 24th February [9th March]. The workers come to the factories in the morning; instead of going to work they hold meetings; then begin processions towards the centre. New districts and new groups of population are drawn towards the movement. The slogan "Bread" is crowded out or obscured by louder slogans: "Down with autocracy!" "Down with the war!". . . . Around the barracks, sentinels, patrols, and lines of soldiers stood groups of working men and women exchanging friendly words with the army men.

(*Source:* L. Trotsky, *The History of the Russian Revolution,* 1932)

Report by an Agent of the Okhrana, 11 March:

The movement which has started has flared up without any party preparing it and without any preliminary discussion of a plan of action . . .

Now everything depends on the behaviour of the military units; if the latter do not join the proletariat, the movement will quickly subside; but if the troops turn against the government, then nothing can save the country from a revolutionary upheaval.

Shulgin, an Octobrist Duma Deputy, Diary Entry for 12 March:

During the last few days we have been living, as it were, on a volcano. . . . It is not, of course, a question of bread. The trouble is that in that large city it is impossible to find a few hundred people who feel kindly towards the government.

There is an unusual degree of unanimity in these accounts, by observers from all points of the political spectrum. Most significantly, all agree on the spontaneity and lack of organized leadership and on the importance of the decision of the garrison troops to defect to the rioters.

Here, perhaps, lies the key to an understanding of 1917. If you think about it, leadership in any institution operates by a system of bluff. Political leaders, army officers, even teachers, are few in numbers; those they command are many. Most of the time people obey those in authority out of habit or out of conviction that it is the best way to get things done. Sometimes, however, this habit of automatic obedience is broken and ordinary people become aware of just how powerful their numbers can be. This is what happened in both civilian life and the armed forces in Russia in 1917. Aspiring political leaders really had no choice but to go along with grass-roots feelings. Those who could not adapt and who retained firm ideas about how the revolution should progress that did not fit in with what the masses wanted were rendered impotent and swept into "the dustbin of history".

REACTIONS TO THE EVENTS OF 8-12 MARCH

Telegram from Nicholas II to General Khabalov, Commander of the Petrograd Military District, 10 March:

I command you to suppress from tomorrow all disorders on the streets of the capital, which are impermissible at a time when the fatherland is carrying on a difficult war with Germany.

Telegram from M. Rodzianko, an Octobrist and President of the State Duma, to Tsar Nicholas II, 12 March:

The situation is serious. There is anarchy in the capital. The government is paralysed. It is necessary immediately to entrust a person who enjoys the confidence of the country with the formation of a government. Any delay is equivalent to death. I pray God that in this hour responsibility will not fall on the sovereign.

Speech by Alexander Kerensky, Socialist Revolutionary, to the Leaders of the Duma, 12 March:

I am constantly receiving information that the troops are agitated. . . . They are coming out on the streets. . . . I am now going to visit the regiments. It is necessary that I should know what to say to them. May I tell them that the State Duma is with them, that it assumes all responsibility [for governing Russia], that it will stand at the head of the movement?

Telegram from General Alekseev, the Commander-in-Chief, to the Commanders of all the Fronts, 15 March:

. . . one of the great revolutions is already in progress; the passions of the populace are difficult to curb; the troops are demoralized . . . the dynastic problem is at stake and the war can be continued to a victorious conclusion only by fulfilling the demands concerning the abdication. . . . The situation does not appear to allow for a different solution. . . . It is imperative to save the field forces from disintegration and to continue fighting our external enemies to the end. . . . This must be our first concern, even at the cost of major concessions.

Nicholas II, Rodzianko, Alekseev and Kerensky came from different social classes, had different backgrounds and philosophies and differed greatly in the extent to which they were in touch with grass-roots feelings. If you think about these differences, it will help you to understand how judgements on the same event can differ so widely.

From 12 March onwards events moved fast.

12 MARCH   The Petrograd Soviet of Workers' and Soldiers' Deputies was formed, a council (the Russian word "soviet" simply means "council") elected by the rank and file in factories and regiments and intended to defend their interests. In the following weeks soviets sprang up all over the country, but the Petrograd one remained the most influential and delegates came to it from all over Russia. Although the Soviet's position was unofficial, it enjoyed enormous prestige among ordinary Russians, and it soon became obvious that no government would be able to function without its co-operation.

Throughout 1917, and especially in the early days, the majority of delegates were ordinary soldiers and workers and the composition of the Soviet served as a barometer of grass-roots feeling. An Executive Committee or Ex-Com, was appointed to run the Soviet's day-to-day affairs. Its size and composition were constantly changing, but members tended to be professional revolutionaries, Mensheviks and Socialist Revolutionaries like Chkeidze, Tsiretelli, Chernov, Sukhanov and Kerensky, rather than ordinary delegates. From the beginning, therefore, there was a risk that the Ex-Com and the main body of the Soviet would look at events from different points of view.

14 MARCH   **Order No. 1 of the Petrograd Soviet issued:**

To the garrison of the Petrograd District. To all the soldiers of the Guard, army, artillery and fleet for immediate and precise execution, and to the workers of Petrograd for information.

The Soviet of Workers' and Soldiers' Deputies has decided:

1. In all companies, battalions, squadrons and separate branches of military service of all kinds and on warships immediately choose committees from elected representatives of the soldiers and sailors of the above-mentioned military units . . .

4. The orders of the military commission of the State Duma are to be fulfilled only in those cases which do not contradict the orders and decisions of the Soviet of Workers' and Soldiers' Deputies.

5. Arms of all kinds . . . must be at the disposition and under the control of the company and battalion committees and are not in any case to be given out to officers, even upon their demand.

6. In the ranks and in fulfilling service duties soldiers must observe the strictest military discipline; but outside of service, in their political, civil and private life, soldiers cannot be discriminated against as regards those rights which all citizens enjoy. Standing at attention and compulsory saluting out of service are especially abolished.

7. In the same way the addressing of officers with titles: Your Excellency, Your Honour etc. is abolished and is replaced by the forms: Mr General, Mr Colonel etc. Rude treatment of soldiers of all ranks and especially addressing them as "thou" is forbidden; and soldiers are obliged to bring to the attention of the company committees any violation of this rule and any misunderstandings between officers and soldiers.

16 MARCH   3 a.m.: Abdication of Tsar Nicholas II in favour of his brother, the Grand Duke Michael.

Mid-morning: After listening to Kerensky's argument that "You will not save Russia by accepting the throne. On the contrary, I know the

A crowd on the streets of Petrograd gleefully burns emblems of the Tsarist Government torn from shop windows and other buildings during the February Revolution – a telling comment on how unpopular the government had become.

sentiments of the mass of soldiers and workers. Bitter dissatisfaction is now directed just against the monarchy", Grand Duke Michael renounced the throne.

The Duma leaders declared the formation of the first Provisional Government, and Russia became a Republic. A cabinet of ministers was appointed. Apart from Kerensky, a moderate socialist who became Minister of Justice, all the others were members of the Kadet and Octobrist parties.

From this series of events you should be able to work out which of the judgements on page 34 proved most accurate. In fact, by 16 March most shrewd politicians of all shades of opinion had accepted Kerensky's view that monarchy could not survive. There was no further consensus, however, on how Russia should develop – socially, economically or politically – after that.

THE VIEW OF THE MIDDLE-CLASS LIBERALS

The First Public Statement of the Provisional Government, published in *Isvestia*, 16 March:

In its present activity the Cabinet will be guided by the following principles:
1. Complete and immediate amnesty for all political and religious cases, including terrorist attacks, military uprisings, agrarian crimes etc.
2. Freedom of speech, press, union, assembly and strikes.
3. Abolition of all caste, religious and national discriminations.
4. Immediate preparation for the convention of a Constituent Assembly, which will establish the form of administration and the constitution of the country, on the basis of general, equal, secret and direct voting . . .
6. Election to the organs of local self-government on the basis of general, direct, equal and secret ballot . . .
8. Along with the maintenance of strict military discipline in the ranks, elimination for soldiers of all limitations of the general rights which are granted to all other citizens.

Appeal by A. Shingarev, Minister for Agriculture, April 1917, published by all leading Russian newspapers, 4 May:

A great disaster threatens our motherland if the population in the rural districts, without waiting for the decision of the Constituent Assembly, itself undertakes the immediate readjustment of land relations. Such arbitrary activities threaten general destruction. The fields will remain unsown and the harvest will not be reaped. Need and hunger will come to the country.

Statement of the Provisional Government, 9 April:
CITIZENS
. . . The country still remains under the attack of a powerful enemy, who has seized whole provinces of our territory and now, in the days of the birth of Russian freedom, threatens us with new decisive attacks. Defence at any cost of our own native land and liberation of the country from the enemy who has invaded its frontiers; this is the first insistent duty of our soldiers, who are defending the liberty of the people . . .

V. Nabakov, a Kadet:

The miraculous swiftness of the coup d'etat, the kind of magical ease with which it toppled at once and totally, the rot-riddled facade of the old order – the genuine enthusiasm that seized everyone, led to unanimous recognition of the new order by the whole country and by Western Europe . . . – all this promised success and prosperity, durability and fruitfulness for the Republic. What happened? No matter in what area of state life we look, nowhere arise irridescent images, but only ominous indications of decay and destruction. The general atmosphere commences to resemble more and more the old, prerevolutionary one. As then, conscientious people who realized what was taking place around them, anxiously asked themselves and each other – What lies ahead? Where is the way out? – so now, too, there is no other question.

(*Source:* from an article published in *Herald of the Party of People's Freedom*, 25 April 1917)

THINGS TO DO AND THINK ABOUT:

Did the Liberals greet the revolution in the streets that gave them power with enthusiasm or trepidation? If they were anxious about the way things were going, can you suggest why this should have been?

What changes in the way Russia was governed did the Government introduce immediately?

What was the Government's policy towards (a) the land, (b) the war? To what extent did these policies differ from those of Nicholas II?

N. Sukhanov, Menshevik Member of Ex-Com, recalls 16 March:

There was laughter [in the Soviet] when someone gave us the information that before his abdication Nicholas had appointed G.E. Lvov Premier. . . . We laughed at the naive anachronism of the text, but didn't pay the slightest attention to the fact of the abdication itself. It was self-evident to all of us that at this point, on March 16th, it introduced absolutely nothing new into the general situation. The Revolution was taking its course, and the new combination of forces would be established quite independently of the activities of any Romanovs.

(*Source:* N. Sukhanov, *The Russian Revolution of 1917. A Personal Record*, O.U.P., 1955)

Statement by the Ex-Com of the Petrograd Soviet on its Relations with the Provisional Government, 28 March:

The Provisional Government is the government of the Revolution and corresponds to the evolutionary level at which Russia now stands. . . . Our task is to aid it in bringing the Revolution to its completion and at the same time to hinder any attempts on its part to retard or turn back the

An English journalist noticed the dramatic change that had taken place in Russian politics in a matter of days.
Left: *the Romanov portrait at the Duma.*
Right: *the Romanov portrait gone and delegates of the Soldiers' Committees in session.*

Revolution. But this second task will also be best achieved not by shouts of betrayal or by attempts at seizure of power by the proletariat, but by an organized pressure on the government and by an indefatigable propagation of our views among the backward section of the population.

This is a rather strange situation. The Soviet is to act as the watchdog of the revolution (against what?) but not to take power itself. From what you have learned about the political theories of the Mensheviks (page 30), this policy of allowing a "bourgeois" government to rule for the foreseeable future should appear quite logical.

There was a further complication in the already confused situation: the Provisional Government had little real authority over the country it was supposed to be leading. Many ministers blamed the Soviet for this state of affairs:

A Letter from Guchkov, Minister for War, to Alekseev, 22 March:

The Provisional Government possesses no real power and its orders are executed only in so far as this is permitted by the Soviet of Workers' and Soldiers' Deputies, which holds in its hands the most important elements of actual power, such as troops, railroads, postal and telegraph service. . . .

Before accepting this assessment at face-value, have another look at that "Order No. 1" that was quoted on page 35. At first glance, it might appear to confirm Guchkov's accusations, but Sukhanov, who witnessed but played no active part in its drafting, throws a different light on the matter:

Around 10 o'clock, going back behind the curtain of Room 13, where the Executive Committee had been in session shortly before, I found the following scene: N.D. Sokolov (Menshevik) was sitting at a table writing. He was surrounded on all sides by soldiers, standing, sitting and leaning on the table, half-dictating and half-suggesting to Sokolov what he should write. . . . There was no agenda and no discussion of any kind, everyone spoke . . . formulating their collective opinion without voting. I stood and listened, extraordinarily interested. When the work was finished they put a heading on the sheet: Order No. 1. This is the background of the document that earned such resounding fame.

(*Source:* from Sukhanov's recollections of 14 March 1917 in *The Russian Revolution of 1917. A Personal Record*, O.U.P., 1955)

If you re-read Order No. 1 carefully, you may conclude that the chaotic circumstances of its composition are clearly reflected in the awkward wording of some of the clauses. More importantly, Sukhanov's recollection indicates that, even in the early days of the revolution, the moderate socialists of the Ex-Com had little control over their rank and file and were sometimes forced to support policies they considered too radical. The Government's weakness, therefore, was not caused by the Soviet leadership but reflected the realization by the masses that they had the power to dictate events.

The Revolution Deepens, April–July 1917

Resolution by the All-Russian Congress of Soviets, 12 May 1917:

As long as the war continues, the Russian democracy recognizes that the downfall of the army . . . would be the heaviest blow to the cause of freedom and to the vital interests of the country. . . . Therefore the Congress of the Soviet of Workers' and Soldiers' Deputies call on the democratic forces in Russia to mobilize all the vital forces of the country in all the spheres of its national life to reinforce the front and the rear.

Isvestia, 27 May 1917:

Thus the new Provisional Government is not going to undertake the final resolution of the question of transferring land to the . . . workers. It is leaving this decision to the Constituent Assembly.
Is this the right thing to do? . . . Would it not be better to give at once to the peasants all the state . . . , monastery, and privately-owned lands? . . . One must bear in mind [the] irregular, uneven land distribution in the country when the land question is being settled. In all fairness, this question can be solved in no other way than *for the whole country simultaneously*. If we start settling the land question by separate volosts, uezds or guberniyas (units of local government), we will achieve nothing but disturbances and new injustices.

There were, of course, considerable philosophical differences between the socialist policies quoted above and those of the liberal ministers of the Provisional Government outlined on pages 36-37. Do you think, however, that to war-weary troops, land-hungry peasants or to urban workers, faced with bread shortages and demands that they work long hours in the factories to meet the needs of the army, socialist policies would have looked substantially different *in practice* from those of the Government?

Before you make up your mind, consider the following indications of what the ordinary people of Russia felt about the issues of bread, peace and land in the early months of the revolution.

THE SOLDIER AT THE FRONT

"Until the end", croaks the crow, picking the human bones on the battlefield. What does he care about the old mother who awaits the return of her son or the octogenarian who with trembling hands leads the plough?
"War to the end", cries the student to thousands of people on the public square and assures them that our hardships are due to the Germans. During this time, his father, who has sold oats at 16 roubles a pood, sits in a noisy cabaret where he maintains the same ideas.
"To the end", clamour the agents of the allied governments while touring the battlefields strewn with the bodies of proletarians. Can the soldier in the trenches cry "War to the end"? No. He says something else.

Until the end of the war, we'll be without food.
Until the end of the war, Russia won't be free.
Comrades, let him who cries "War to the end" be sent to the front lines.
Then we'll see what he says.

(*Source:* Article in the newspaper, *Citizen Soldier*, April 1917)

THE WORKERS

Message from Railway Workers of the Archangel Line to the Moscow Soviet, March 1917:

It remains now to create a new life founded on law and equity. Minister Kerensky, we ask you to consider that if we address ourselves to you to tell of our complaints, it's because we can't stand any more.

Petition presented to Petrograd Soviet by the Working Women of Ekaterinodar, March 1917:

We work up to ten and a half hours a day and some of us are paid only 1 rouble 20 kopecks. We are forced to undergo a degrading search. There are no facilities whatever for our meals or for cleaning up. We want:
    8 hour day
    Wages by the day, not piece-rate
    Wages for working women of 3 roubles a day
    No more searches
    Installation of canteen and toilet facilities
    Boiling water for meals . . .
    Management to be polite to workers
    No discharge without approval of "factory committee"
    Weekly payment of wages
    2 weeks' pay in case of dismissal . . .

Complaint made to Sukhanov by his Friend's Housekeeper, 17 April:

The queues – well the queues haven't got any smaller in the least; I think they're even bigger. You stand half the day just as before. . . . They say "libberty-flibberty, it's all the same, there's nothing to be had". They say it's just the same, "the rich keep on fleecing the poor. The shopkeepers are the only ones making money".

(*Source:* N. Sukhanov, *The Russian Revolution of 1917. A Personal Record*, O.U.P., 1955)

THE PEASANTS

Resolution presented to the Congress of Peasant Deputies by a Delegation from Kursk Province, 17 May:

The right of private property in land is to be abolished for ever; land can neither be bought nor sold nor leased nor pledged nor alienated in any way. All land . . . is taken over without compensation as the property of the whole people and passes over to the use of those who work on it. . . . The right of using the land is enjoyed by all citizens (without distinction of sex) of the Russian state who desire to cultivate it with their own labour, with the help of their family, or in a co-operative group, and only so long as they are able to cultivate it.

This was typical of hundreds of resolutions submitted by rural areas.

LENIN   There were some who realized the implications of the gulf between the demands of the masses and the principles of the socialist politicians. Consider this extract from a series of letters sent by personal messenger from Zürich in Switzerland to the Bolshevik Party in Petrograd between 7 and 22 March:

> The first stage of the Revolution has ended. This first stage will certainly not be the last stage of our revolution. . . . The imperialist war with objective inevitability had to hasten extraordinarily and to sharpen in unprecedented fashion the class war of the proletariat against the bourgeoisie, had to turn into a civil war between hostile classes. . . . The government of Octobrists and Kadets, of Guchkovs and Milyukovs can give neither peace nor bread nor freedom.
>
> (*Source:* V. Lenin, *Letters from Afar*, Vol. 5)

Over a decade before, Lenin had rejected the orthodox Marxist view that Tsarism must be followed by a period of bourgeois government, and had advocated an immediate seizure of power by the proletariat (see page 31). Now, at last, he saw an opportunity to put theory into practice. While Liberals, Mensheviks and Socialist Revolutionaries sought to persuade the masses that the hardships of war must be endured, Lenin urged those Bolsheviks already in Russia to stir up discontent into class war and prepare for a seizure of power by the proletariat.

If things had worked out differently in 1917, his letters might well have been dismissed as the ravings of a fanatic. With the benefit of hindsight, can you see how important they are? In the early weeks following the February Revolution, the Bolsheviks in Petrograd, who edited the party newspaper *Pravda*, adopted the Menshevik line of limited co-operation with the Provisional Government. Without Lenin's urging, this attitude might never have changed and the November Revolution might never have taken place.

When Lenin wrote these letters, however, he had no idea of how he was actually going to get back to Russia from his place of exile in Zürich, and put the Bolshevik Party on the right track. Between Switzerland and Russia lay Germany and Austria-Hungary, with whom Russia was still at war. A solution was eventually found when the Germans granted permission for Lenin and his fellow exiles to cross Germany to the Baltic coast by special "sealed" train, on condition that they did not try to communicate with the German public along the way and infect them with revolutionary ideas. From Sassnitz on the Baltic, the party caught a boat to neutral Sweden and then travelled by train via Finland to Petrograd.

In July 1917 Lenin's opponents were to turn this incident against him, as part of a campaign to blacken his reputation. It proved, they were to argue, that the Bolsheviks were paid agents of the Germans, hired to take Russia out of the war. The accusations were highly embarrassing for Lenin. He could hardly deny the manner of his homecoming, nor that he intended to end Russian involvement in the war, but he did strenuously deny that he had ever accepted German money. It has since been proved that Lenin lied on this point, and that German money found its way into Bolshevik Party funds before and after the February Revolution. This did not necessarily mean that Lenin and the German Government were collaborating in any ordinary sense of the word. They may well have been *using* each other for their own quite separate ends, although Lenin must have felt in July 1917 that ordinary Russians would misunderstand his motives.

Lenin arrived at Petrograd's Finland Station on 16 April and made an impromptu speech to assembled party workers. The main points of his arguments were developed in more detail in the April Theses.

Extracts from the April Theses, published in *Pravda*, 20 April 1917:

1. In our attitude towards the war, which on Russia's side, also under the new government of Lvov and Co, remains a predatory imperialistic war as a result of the capitalist character of this government, not the least concessions to "revolutionary defensism" are permissible . . .
Organization of the most widespread propaganda for the viewpoint in the army in the field . . . Fraternization . . .
3. No support for the Provisional Government, explanation of the complete falsity of all its promises.
4. Explanation to the masses that the Soviet of Workers' and Soldiers' Deputies is the sole possible form of revolutionary government . . . all state power should pass into its hands, so that the masses by experience should free themselves from mistakes . . .
6. Confiscation of all land belonging to landlords.

The Theses are really a list of instructions for Bolshevik party members on how they should organize their propaganda. Soldiers at the front should be taught that they are fighting only for the interests of the bourgeoisie and encouraged to abandon the war and fraternize with the ordinary German soldiers. (Lenin believed that a successful proletarian revolution in Russia would soon be followed by a similar one in Germany.) Loyalty to the Provisional Government should be undermined and the masses urged to demand a transfer of power to the soviets. Peasant support should be recruited by the promise of immediate land reform.

You may have noticed that there appears to be something of a contradiction in Lenin's argument. He called for a transfer of power to the soviets as the most effective way of handing power over to the working people. The soviets, however, were under the control of moderate socialists who refused to take power and saw the Provisional Government as the natural successor to the Tsar. One of the party's priorities, therefore, would have to be to win a Bolshevik majority in the soviets, and to do this they needed some sort of simple mass appeal. In the months that followed the Bolsheviks adopted the catchy slogans: "Bread, peace and land" and "All Power to the Soviets".

REACTIONS TO LENIN IN APRIL 1917

This is the raving of a madman! It's indecent to applaud this clap-trap. You ought to be ashamed of yourselves! Call yourselves Marxists?

(*Source:* Heckling by Bogdanov, Menshevik, Chairman of the Ex-Com, when Lenin addressed the Soviet, 17 April)

In yesterday's issue of "Pravda" Comrade Lenin published his theses. They represent the *personal* opinion of Comrade Lenin . . .

As regards Comrade Lenin's general line, it appears to us unacceptable inasmuch as it proceeds from the assumption that the bourgeois-democratic revolution *has been completed* and it builds on the immediate transformation of this revolution into a Socialist revolution. The tactics that follow from such analysis are greatly at variance with the tactics defended by the representatives of "Pravda".

(*Source:* from an article "Our Differences" by L. Kamenev, a fellow Bolshevik, published in *Pravda*, 21 April 1917)

It is hardly surprising that the initial reaction of the Mensheviks was one of shock. After all, Lenin's call for an immediate transfer of power to the proletariat was hardly in line with orthodox Marxism and difficult for other Marxists to swallow. Kamenev's objections may seem more surprising, as he had been a close friend of Lenin's before 1917. It seems, however, that many Bolsheviks had not really taken Lenin's idea of an *immediate* socialist revolution very seriously and it took them some time to adjust to the new Party line.

What do the events of March and April 1917 tell us about Lenin as a man and a politician?

CHANGES IN THE PROVISIONAL GOVERNMENT

The view of the Provisional Government: the war must go on. War Minister Kerensky addresses troops in the hope of instilling enthusiasm for a summer offensive.

In May significant changes took place in the Provisional Government. There were three new ministers:

Chernov (Socialist Revolutionary)   Minister for Agriculture
Tseretelli (Menshevik)   Minister for Posts and Telegraph
Skobelev (Menshevik)   Minister for Labour

Kerensky, Minister for Justice in the outgoing administration, was promoted to Minister for War. The Provisional Government was now also sometimes called the first Coalition Government.

Declaration of the Provisional Government, 19 May:

Reorganized and strengthened by new representatives of the revolutionary democracy, the Provisional Government . . . is especially united by the following basic principles in its future activity:
1. In foreign policy the Provisional Government, rejecting, in agreement with the whole people, any thought of a separate peace, openly sets as its goal the speediest achievement of a general peace, which does not have as its objective dominion over other peoples, of taking away from them their national possessions or violent seizure of foreign territories – a peace without annexations . . . on the basis of self-determination of the peoples . . .

2. Convinced that the defeat of Russia and its allies would not only be a source of the greatest sufferings of the peoples, but would postpone or make impossible the conclusion of a general peace on the above-mentioned basis, the Provisional Government firmly believes that the revolutionary army of Russia will not permit the enemy to crush our Allies in the West and to turn with all its arms against us . . .

5. Leaving to the Constituent Assembly the solution of the problem of transferring the land to the possession of the toilers . . . the Provisional Government will take all measures which are necessary to assure the greatest production of bread for the country . . .

The changes of personnel were intended to increase the Government's popularity with the masses. From what you already know about the politics of the Mensheviks and Socialist Revolutionaries in 1917 and from an examination of the manifesto of 19 May, do you think there are likely to be any significant changes in the direction of the Government's policies?

In fact, from May onwards, Government policy statements and those of the Soviet Ex-Com became increasingly indistinguishable and these had altered little from those quoted earlier for March and April 1917. Land redistribution and improvements in urban working conditions must wait at least until the convening of the Constituent Assembly, whose election date was constantly postponed because of the very real difficulties involved in holding democratic elections in war-time. The war itself must continue until Germany consented to make peace on the principles of 19 May. Stalemate!

Voting with their feet. By the summer of 1917 desertion from the army was so common that there was no need for secrecy.

Government and Soviet leaders had now to persuade the masses that the above policies were fair and feasible and that they must make enormous sacrifices for the foreseeable future. Could this be done? Judge for yourself from the following:

THE SOLDIERS   **General Brusilov at a Conference of Commanders, May 1917:**

I tried persuasion on the mutineers and for a long time. But when I asked them whether they agreed with me, they asked leave to give me a written answer, and in a few minutes they put before my eyes a poster reading, "Peace at any price, down with the war!" When we began to talk again, one of them declared, "Since 'without annexations and contributions' is to be the word, what value for us has that hill over there?" I replied, "That hill is worth nothing to me either. But we have got to fight the enemy who is holding it". Finally they gave me their word that they would not withdraw. But they refused to advance. "Our enemies are good fellows", they said. "They told us they would not advance if we did not. We want to go home, to enjoy our liberty and use our land. Why should we get ourselves crippled?"

THE PEASANTS   **Report by a Representative from Penza Province to the Agrarian Committee in Petrograd, July 1917:**

Imagine what it is like in our province, with peasants so poor that they have only a few sazhens each; how can a man with a wife and three children live like that? It is no surprise that, with such small plots, the peasants wanted to improve their lot as soon as liberty was proclaimed, not only in their dignity but also in their conditions now that Tsarism, which everyone said was the cause of their misfortunes has been swept away. It was for this reason that, following the decisions of our regional soviet on 15 May, the peasants have changed land ownership even before the meeting of the constituent assembly to legalize its decisions. . . . That is how the land of the proprietors, towns, monasteries, dynasty and the like came to be managed by local committees, which then shared them out among needy workers. That is what happened to sacrosanct private property.

THE WORKERS   **Message to the Provisional Government from the Riga Office of the State Bank, 12 May:**

A completely inimical attitude towards the Liberty Loan [a voluntary subscription towards the war effort] was demonstrated by the council of the Riga labour organizations; the reason given was that the loan would go for the goal of war, while the war is up to now and continues to be an aggressive war.

It is important to note that the issues above interlinked. As long as the war over-strained the transport system, conditions in the cities would continue to deteriorate. In the conditions of shortage prices rose quickly.

Bread Rations:

	March	April	September	October
Manual workers	1½ lbs per day	¾ lb per day	½ lb per day	¼ lb per day
Others	1 lb per day	¾ lb per day	½ lb per day	¼ lb per day

In the cities, the continuation of the war meant ever-lengthening bread queues.

Selected Food Prices, 1917:

	July	October
Lard (1 lb)	1-10 roubles	5-40 roubles
Cheese (1 lb)	1-60 roubles	5-40 roubles
Cabbage (1 lb)	1-60 roubles	2-20 roubles
Sausages (1 lb)	1-00 roubles	6-00 roubles

The war was not completely to blame. With some monthly fluctuations, the figures for food supplies to the cities tended to worsen steadily throughout the year. As legal land repartition was delayed and the peasants increasingly took matters into their own hands, normal agriculture was disrupted and food production fell. Rural chaos also affected the army; as news of land seizures reached the front, soldiers deserted en masse for their native villages, to join in the share-out, and made nonsense of the idea of continuing the war till victory. On the other hand, hardships in the towns triggered off a dramatic decrease in industrial production, thus further diminishing the chances of a successful outcome to the war and increasing the disaffection of the army. None of these problems could really be solved in isolation from the others.

THE BOLSHEVIKS Lenin and the Bolsheviks set themselves the task of exploiting discontent in order to bring about a second and more radical revolution.

A Bolshevik Sergeant to his Regiment, July 1917:

Comrades! For 300 years the bourgeois and the landlords drank your blood! Now we have overthrown the Tsarist regime, but are we free? Not at all! Instead of the Tsarist government we have Kerensky. Who is Kerensky? He is a hireling of the Russian and foreign bourgeoisie!

Kerensky forces you to continue this senseless, criminal war. Do you need this bloody, criminal war? . . . Do you want to shed your blood for the interests of the English and American capitalists? . . . Do you want peace? . . . Listen, Kerensky, the Mensheviks and the Socialist Revolutionaries are betraying the working people; they have sold themselves to the English and American bourgeoisie, that is why they want to send you into battle again and again. Only our party, the Bolshevik Party, will give you peace.

Resolution presented by Lenin at the All-Russian Congress of Peasants' Deputies, 15 June:

1. All lands belonging to landowners and other private proprietors as well as . . . church lands etc., must be immediately turned over, without compensation, to the people.
2. The peasantry must seize all the lands immediately, in an organized manner, through their Soviets of Peasants' Deputies, and manage them economically . . .
3. Private ownership in land must be generally abolished, i.e. the right of ownership of all the lands must be vested in the people as a whole; the management of the land, however, must rest with local democratic institutions . . .

In such a chaotic political situation it is almost impossible to assess accurately how much support the Bolsheviks had actually built up by early July. We have some pieces of the puzzle but not enough to complete the whole picture. At the first All-Russian Congress of Soviets, which opened on 16 June, the delegates were as follows:

Socialist Revolutionaries	285
Mensheviks	248
Bolsheviks	105
Other socialists	105

Lenin's resolution calling for the conversion of the world war into a class war was defeated by 126 votes to 543.

Three days earlier, however, on 13 June, the Bolsheviks had won a majority in the workers' section of the Petrograd Soviet, although this did not yet constitute a majority in the Soviet as a whole. At this point it would seem that the Bolsheviks were more influential in the cities than in the country as a whole, and for a party planning revolution this was encouraging news. In a revolutionary situation political power is not simply a matter of winning votes. It is also about control of crucial sectors of the economy and the armed forces. 10,000 armed factory workers may be more use in overthrowing a government than the votes of a million peasants.

Moreover, time was on the side of the Bolsheviks. While the Government and the Soviet Ex-Com pursued unpopular policies, the trend of support away from the moderate socialists was likely to continue. Lenin seems to have understood this well. Traditionally, the Bolsheviks were the party of the urban proletariat, but we have seen that Lenin was already making a determined bid for the support of the army and peasantry as well.

SUMMARY If the Provisional Government was to maintain power and fulfil its proclaimed aim of guiding Russia to democracy, it had some complex problems to solve. These were the options open to the Government at the beginning of July 1917:

1. The Government could use traditional methods to try to restore law and order. Troops could be sent to pacify the countryside, traditional discipline be restored at the front and the police ordered to bring the towns and factories back under control. This line of action was advocated by some generals. Do you think it had any chance of being effective?
2. The Government could outlaw the Bolsheviks. This was a popular suggestion among non-socialist politicians. It would only work, of course, if the Bolsheviks were the main cause of popular disaffection and were not merely taking advantage of a situation that already existed.
3. The Government could try to persuade the ordinary people that its policies of discipline in the factories, postponement of land reform and continuation of the war were in their own best interests. This was the policy actually tried. War Minister Kerensky toured the front throughout June, attempting to whip up enthusiasm for an offensive among the troops. He was nicknamed contemptuously by old-fashioned generals "Persuader-in-Chief". It did not work.

THINGS TO DO AND THINK ABOUT:

Was there some other solution to the Government's dilemma? Think about what might have happened had Russia withdrawn from the war. This course might have provided a breathing-space during which the Government could begin to tackle Russia's formidable domestic problems, but there were considerable risks involved. Draw up a list of the pros and cons of this option, remembering that we can never know what really would have happened.

Lenin has made some sweeping promises – land to the peasants and bread to the towns – and we are justified in wondering how easily he would be able to fulfil both these promises at once. Can you work out what sort of problems he might encounter? It is easier to win power than to hold it.

Revolution and Counter-Revolution, July–September 1917

Let us now return to the actual course of events in Russia from the beginning of July 1917. On 2 July the Russian army launched an offensive on the Austrian Front which collapsed after several days with a massive loss of life. A fortnight later an incident known as the "July Days" occurred, around which controversy still rages.

THE JULY DAYS

On 16 and 17 July armed demonstrators – workers, garrison soldiers and sailors from the Kronstadt naval base – marched to the headquarters of the Soviet at the Tauride Palace. Here is an example of their demands:

Statement of the Representatives of 54 Factories to the Executive Committee of the Petrograd Soviet, 17 July:

We demand the withdrawal of the ten capitalist ministers. We trust the Soviet, but not those whom the Soviet trusts [members of the Provisional Government from the Kadet and Octobrist parties]. Our comrades, the Socialist Ministers, entered into an agreement with the capitalists, but these capitalists are our mortal enemies. We demand that the land should be seized immediately, that control over industry should be seized immediately. . . . The will of the democracy is quite clear; the transfer of power into the hands of the Soviet.

The Soviet Reply:

We protest against these evil signs of indiscipline, which undermine any form of government by the people, not excepting the future government of the Constituent Assembly. We demand once and for all a stoppage of such outbreaks which disgrace revolutionary Petrograd.

(*Source:* Resolution of 17 July adopted by the Executive Committee in conjunction with the uprising which began on 16 July)

Think carefully about what the demonstrators were asking for. They assumed that it was only the presence of non-socialists in the Provisional Government that was preventing the whole-hearted adoption of policies embodying the will of the ordinary people. If the Soviet seized power immediately, all would be well. From what we already know about the socialists of the Ex-Com, do you think the workers' expectations were realistic? Are you surprised at the Soviet's response or would you argue that they could hardly have been expected to react otherwise?

This mini-revolution collapsed quickly, for the Provisional Government was not yet so discredited that it could not muster sufficient loyal regiments. Official blame for the outbreak was placed squarely on the Bolsheviks. Those who did not arrange to disappear quickly enough were arrested; Lenin fled in disguise to Finland; the Bolshevik press was closed down and the Government published documents purporting to prove that the Bolsheviks were in regular receipt of German money and were being paid to take Russia out of the war.

The question of whether the Bolsheviks were seriously trying to seize power during the July Days is tricky to answer. In his history of the revolution, written in the 1930s, Trotsky argued that "the movement had begun from below, irrespective of the Bolsheviks – to a certain extent against their will". Trotsky's denial cannot be accepted unsupported (can you work out why not?), but more objective evidence exists that supports his view.

Firstly, eye-witnesses of all shades of opinion noticed the lack of centralized and co-ordinated planning during the demonstrations. This was in marked contrast to the very efficient way in which the Bolsheviks were to organize the November Revolution. Secondly, the Bolsheviks did not yet have a majority in the Petrograd Soviet, which, from their point of view, made nonsense of the July slogan, "All power to the Soviets". And, thirdly, Trotsky went to the rescue of Chernov, the Minister for Agriculture, who was being menaced by the demonstrators. He took the opportunity to make a speech pleading with the crowd to disperse.

One last question remains. If the Bolsheviks were so lukewarm about the demonstrations, why did they not condemn them outright? The most likely answer is that the Bolsheviks feared that they would lose popular support if they disassociated themselves too strongly from what was obviously a popular movement and so tried to play it both ways.

The Provisional Government hoped that the events of July would turn the tide of popular support away from the Bolsheviks and for a few weeks it seemed as if this might be happening. To win the Government further approval the socialist, Kerensky, was appointed Prime Minister on 21 July. However, would reaction against the Bolsheviks halt the growing alienation of the disgruntled masses from the official Government? Once again, before we investigate what happened next, let us look at Russia at grass-roots level in the late summer and autumn of 1917.

THE PEASANTS

Outbreaks of Violence in Selected Rural Areas (mainly illegal land seizures, burning of landlords' property etc):

	July-August	September-October
Tula	66	162
Ryazan	60	165
Saratov	35	145
Penza	104	184
Tambov	90	281
Minsk	76	199

Government pleas to await the decision of the Constituent Assembly over land redistribution were greeted by peasants with growing impatience. Many villages formed revolutionary detachments to seize land from neighbouring landlords, and deserters from the army often joined in.

THE SOLDIERS

Letter from an Anonymous Soldier to the Petrograd Soviet, 22 August:

In the trenches I read the newspaper . . . they discuss war, discipline, punishments, occupation for soldiers etc . . . all that is good for the bourgeois . . . but why should they talk about "fatherland in danger", all the Kerenskys, Skobelevs and Chernovs. . . . Nicholas II could talk that way but not them. . . . Be warned that if peace hasn't come by winter, you can pack your bags. . . . You have betrayed Russian soldiers to England and France.

THE WORKERS Resolution of Workers' Section of Petrograd Soviet, 25 September:

The Government will go down in the history of the Revolution as the Government of the civil war. The Soviet declares: "We, the workers and garrison of Petersburg refuse to support the Government of bourgeois autocracy and counter-revolutionary violence. We express the unshakable conviction that the new Government will meet with a single response from the entire revolutionary democracy: "Resign!"

THE GENERALS There were other, equally disillusioned groups in Russia. Those army officers who had tolerated the abolition of the monarchy in the hope that it would produce an upsurge of patriotism were soon disappointed. With the breakdown of traditional authority, they had been stripped of their power to influence events and had little choice but to live – in varying degrees of discomfort – with the situation in which they found themselves. This is why members of the old ruling class have so far played so small a role in the events covered by book. With the failure of the July offensive, however, the generals seem to have felt that a crisis-point had been reached.

Report by General Klembovsky at a Conference of Generals at Moghilev, July 1917:

The Northern Front is in a condition of dissolution. Not a single officer's order is fulfilled without begging and humiliation before the soldiers. Fraternizing goes on everywhere; if machine guns are turned against the fraternizers mobs of soldiers throw themselves on the guns and make them useless. . . . What can help? The death sentence? But can you really hang whole divisions? Courts martial? But then half the army will be in Siberia. You don't frighten the soldier with imprisonment at hard-labour. "Hard labour? Well, what of it?" they say. "I'll return in five years. At any rate, I'll have a whole skin".

Speech by General Kornilov, Commander-in-Chief, 28 August:

In order to restore the army, the Provisional Government must immediately adopt the measures that I have proposed in a report . . . Historical inferences and combat experience show that there can be no army without discipline. Only an army welded by iron discipline, only an army that is led by the single, inflexible will of its leaders, only such an army is capable of achieving victory and is worthy of victory. . .

Discipline must be affirmed in the daily routine work of the army by vesting the superiors, the officers, the non-commissioned officers with corresponding authority.

There is no disagreement here about facts, but a fundamental divergence of opinion over the possibility of dealing effectively with the problems.

THE KORNILOV AFFAIR On 3 September the Germans captured Riga, an important Russian port on the Baltic. A week later Kornilov issued a proclamation:

Russian People,
Our great Motherland is perishing.
The final hour is near.
Compelled to come out openly, I, General Kornilov, declare that the
Provisional Government under the pressure of the Bolshevik majority in
the soviets, acts in full agreement with the plans of the German General
Staff . . . destroys the army and upsets the country from within. The
painful consciousness of the inevitable destruction of the country
commands me at this threatening moment to summon all Russian people
to save the perishing motherland. . . . I, General Kornilov, the son of a
Cossack peasant, declare to all that personally I want nothing except the
preservation of Great Russia, and I vow to bring the people through
victory over the enemy, to the Constituent Assembly, at which the people
will itself decide its own form of government. I cannot betray Russia into
the hands of its historic enemy, the German tribe, and make the Russian
people slaves of the Germans.
KORNILOV

*The mood of the army,
September 1917.
Kornilov's troops fraternize
with pro-Bolshevik soldiers
sent out from Petrograd
and their advance peters
out.*

On the same day, the general ordered the Cossack regiments under his
command to march on Petrograd in order to suppress the Soviet,
reconstruct the Provisional Government and restore law and order at the
front and in the cities. Although they set out as ordered, the Cossacks soon
mutinied and refused to go any further. Meanwhile, in Petrograd, Kerensky,
apparently in a panic, called on the Bolsheviks to organize the defence of
the capital and armed their private army, the Red Guard, from public
munition stocks – 20,000 rifles, which the Bolsheviks never returned.

If we are to understand what happened during those chaotic few days known as the "Kornilov Affair", there are a number of issues to consider. Even then, the evidence may not be unambiguous enough for every question to be answered conclusively. First of all, Kornilov claims that the dissolution of the army is leaving the country open to German invasion and that responsibility for this lies with the Soviet, controlled by the Bolsheviks, who are in German pay. Willingly or unwillingly (Kornilov is vague on this point), the Provisional Government is but a stooge of these evil forces. The causes of the disaster at Riga were quite clear in Kornilov's mind. Was Kornilov's analysis a genuine and honest attempt to come to grips with Russia's problems or was it a pretext for other, less honourable motives? Even the general's bitterest critics such as the Bolshevik, Trotsky, do not substantially disagree with the verdict that he was an honest, if vain, man attempting to do his duty as he interpreted it.

Kornilov argued afterwards that he had begun preparations for his coup with the connivance of Kerensky, who was afraid of growing Bolshevik popularity, and that Kerensky had backed out at the last moment, leaving Kornilov alone. Thus, continued the general, he was guilty of rebellion only in a technical and not in a moral sense. This interpretation was strenuously denied by the Prime Minister. Neither testimony can be accepted at face value, for both men had reasons for presenting events in a particular light.

The most important questions have been left until last. Does all this really matter all that much? Kornilov believed that his Cossacks could turn the course of history, but if you study the 9 September proclamation closely you may conclude that the Commander-in-Chief had totally misjudged what was happening in Russia. Was it really the Bolsheviks who made the country ungovernable or the Russian people themselves? If you compare Kornilov's assessment with that of the more sophisticated Klembovsky, it is difficult to avoid the conclusion that Kornilov really was the politically naive soldier whom one of his colleagues had once described as having "the heart of a lion and the brain of a lamb". In other words, the Kornilov Affair, however instigated, never stood the least chance of success.

Is the Kornilov Affair worth studying at all, except as a footnote in the history books? In the many thousands of pages he wrote after 1917, justifying his own behaviour, Kerensky certainly thought so, arguing that the summer months had seen a dramatic decline in the Bolshevik influence in the factories and at the front and that this trend had been reversed by the Kornilov Affair. There is a case to be made, however, for the opinion that even without Kornilov the July Days would have been but a hiccup in the rising tide of Bolshevik popularity. All we can say with certainty is that the events of September *were* advantageous to Lenin's party, for ordinary Russians, already disillusioned with the results of the February Revolution, were unlikely to waste much thought on the "truth" of what had happened. They judged events in the light of the way they already felt about the Provisional Government, the generals and the Bolsheviks, and listened to propaganda in a highly selective way. When the Bolsheviks cried that counter-revolution threatened and that only they could save the revolution, there were many ready to believe them, and the party must have won many converts in September. The extent to which this would have happened anyway is impossible to disentangle.

On the Eve: October/November 1917

Bolshevik Party Membership, 1917:

	April	August
Total membership	80,000	200,000
Number of local organizations	78	162
Petrograd Party membership	16,000	36,000

(*Source:* reported by Sverdlov and Volodarsky at 6th Party Congress held in Petrograd 8-16 August)

Bolshevik Groups in the Army:

	July	September	November
South-Western Front	44	108	135
Rumanian Front	30	65	145

Moscow Municipal Elections, 1917:

	July	October
Socialist Revolutionaries	374,885 (58%)	54,374 (14%)
Mensheviks	76,407 (12%)	15,887 (4%)
Bolsheviks	75,409 (11%)	198,320 (51%)
Kadets	108,781 (17%)	101,106 (26%)

19 SEPTEMBER Bolsheviks won an overall majority in the Moscow Soviet.

6 OCTOBER Bolsheviks won an overall majority in the Petrograd Soviet.

The first stage of Lenin's plan had been fulfilled. If power were transferred to the Soviets now, it would be equivalent to handing over power to the Bolshevik Party and the classes that supported it. The party had to decide where to proceed from here. Lenin proposed:

Having obtained the majority in the Soviet of Workers' and Soldiers' Deputies in both capitals the Bolsheviki can and must take the state power into their hands. . . . An insurrection must rest on a turning point in the history of a growing revolution, when the activity of the leading ranks of the people is greatest, and when the wavering in the ranks of the enemies and of the weak, half-hearted friends of the revolution are greatest.

(*Source:* Letter to the Central Committee of the Bolshevik Party from his hiding place at Viborg, near Petrograd)

Lenin's proposal was defeated in the Central Committee by 4 votes to 6, with 6 abstaining.

Up to now we have tended to discuss Bolshevik Party affairs as if Lenin's will was synonymous with that of the party and his word law. What does this incident reveal about Lenin's true position among the Bolsheviks?

20 OCTOBER   Lenin returned to Petrograd.

23 OCTOBER   Meeting of the Party Central Committee with Lenin attending. We have no first-hand minutes of the course of the debate, but the following documents emerged from the meeting:

23 October Resolution of the Central Committee of the Bolshevik Party in favour of Armed Uprising:

The Central Committee recognizes that both the international position of the Russian Revolution (the mutiny in the navy in Germany is an extreme manifestation of the growth throughout Europe of the worldwide socialist revolution) . . . and the acquiring of a majority in the soviets by the proletarian party – all this, combined with the peasant uprising and the turn of popular confidence towards our party (the election in Moscow). . . . All this places armed uprising on the order of the day . . .

24 October Letter from L. Kamenev and G. Zinoviev to the Major Branches of the Bolshevik Party:

It is said: (1) the majority of the people in Russia are already for us and (2) the majority of the international proletariat are for us. Alas! neither one nor the other is true, and this is the crux of the matter.
A majority of workers and a significant part of the army in Russia are for us. But all the rest are in question. We are convinced, for example, that if it now comes to elections to the Constituent Assembly, then the majority of peasants will vote for the SRs. . . . The mass of soldiers supports us not because of our war slogan but because of our peace slogan. . . . If we take power now alone and are forced . . . to wage a revolutionary war, the mass of soldiers will flee from us. . . .
Those same delegates from the front who are now conducting such an agitation against the war are asking our speakers openly not to speak of a revolutionary war because this will put the soldiers off.
. . . And now we come to the second assertion, that supposedly, the majority of the international proletariat are already on our side. This, unfortunately is not true. The uprising in the German fleet had enormous symptomatic significance. The portents exist for a serious movement in Italy. But from there to some degree of active support for the proletarian revolution in Russia . . . is still very far. It is extremely harmful to overrate one's forces . . . if we now lose the battle, having staked everything, we shall inflict a cruel blow also to the international proletarian revolution, growing extremely slowly but none the less without any doubt growing. . .

From what was to happen in November there should be no doubt about who won the debate this time round, but Kamenev and Zinoviev's doubt about whether a socialist revolution can survive for long in backward Russia deserves consideration. There have been many, both contemporaries and historians, who have agreed with the two dissenters.

3 NOVEMBER Creation of Military Revolutionary Committee to co-ordinate tactics. Members of the Committee visited the Kronversk arsenal and seized great quantities of arms and ammunition.

4 NOVEMBER Red Guard, hitherto an impromptu militia, was formalized and organized.

5 NOVEMBER Trotsky successfully appealed to the garrison of the Peter and Paul fortress to put their armaments at the disposal of the Red Guard. Workers at the Sestrorektskii factory handed over 5,000 rifles to the Military Revolutionary Committee.

These events took place in Petrograd, where the history of the November Revolution is best documented. They were repeated, to a greater or lesser extent, in other Russian cities. Few of the preparations were really secret and the Government was well aware of what was going on.

I could pray that such an uprising would take place. I have more strength than I need. They will finally be smashed.

(Kerensky to V. Nabakov, 2 November)

There are no palliative measures for restoring the army's fighting power that are capable of overcoming the destructive influence of the peace propaganda. . . . The only possible way to combat the pernicious influence of the Bolsheviks is to pull the rug out from under them by immediately proposing to make peace ourselves. . . . News of peace negotiations will . . . lay the basis for restoring the army to health. By relying on the units that remain most intact we would find it possible to forcibly suppress anarchy in the countryside.

(*Source:* rough notes made by General Verkovsky for a report to be drafted for a cabinet meeting to be held on 2 November)

It should be obvious by now whose judgement was to prove the more accurate. Kerensky refused to listen to Verkovsky's report and sent him on indefinite leave.

SUMMARY This brings us back to 6 November 1917, where this book opened. You should now have a clearer grasp of why individuals and groups reacted as they did to the Bolshevik coup. Aspects that you need to consider in the light of your new understanding are: 1. The enthusiasm with which the industrial proletariat and some of the soldiers fought for the Bolshevik cause; 2. The indifference of the rest of the soldiery, especially the front-line regiments, to the fate of the Provisional Government; 3. The rigidity with which Mensheviks and Socialist Revolutionaries stuck to their policies over the war and land redistribution, even when the more shrewd among them realized that they were losing mass support to the Bolsheviks.

Epilogue

In 1963 a French historian, Marc Ferro, interviewed the Russian ex-Prime Minister, Kerensky, then 77 years old.

FERRO – How do you account for [Lenin's] success?
KERENSKY – Demagogy, the Bolsheviks promised the moon, but they got a civil war; land to the peasants, but the food was taken away; workers' self-management, which didn't last six months; more liberties still, and Lenin abolished them one after the other.

There is justification for Kerensky's accusations. Within three months of the October Revolution, the new government had issued the following decrees: 8 November – Decree on Land; 26 November – Decree establishing worker-control over all industrial enterprises; 28 January 1918 – Decree authorizing volunteer-Red Army run on democratic lines, including the election of officers by committees of the rank and file. Within three years, however, a highly disciplined, traditionally-run Red Army had replaced the concept of the "armed people"; democratically-elected soviets had been replaced by soviets controlled by Communist Party officials; a secret police – the Cheka – suppressed not only class enemies but political dissidents from the working class as well; the right of peasants to the free use of their land had been replaced by the forced requisitioning of grain for the Red Army. How can this rapid transition from total democracy to rigid dictatorship be explained? There are two views on this.

Throughout 1917 Lenin argued that the masses were mature enough for political responsibility. Others disagreed, arguing that the masses equated Bolshevism with immediate gratification and would fail to realize that sacrifices would be necessary to protect the revolution against the propertied classes. To stay in power, therefore, the Bolsheviks would be forced to establish an iron dictatorship.

Others lay the blame on the civil war which broke out in the summer of 1918. For three years the Whites – Russian opponents of Bolshevism, ranging from supporters of the Tsar to Menshevik politicians who had been Lenin's comrades in exile, and supported by Russia's former allies, Britain and France – fought to oust the Bolsheviks from power. Only in 1921 was the last White army driven from Russian soil.

The two verdicts may not be very far apart. It was predictable that those dispossessed by the revolution would eventually fight back and it can be argued that Lenin seriously misjudged the temper of ordinary Russians when he assumed that they would fight a civil war with enthusiasm. The conclusion you come to over this issue is a matter for your own personal judgement.

As a result, the Soviet state that emerged from the civil war in 1921 little resembled that which had been envisaged in 1917. Some idealistic communists regarded this as a betrayal. The Kronstadt sailors, for example, long a mainstay of the communist regime, issued a series of demands in March 1921, which were intended to replace party dictatorship with working-class democracy:

Demands of the Kronstadt Sailors:

1. In view of the fact that the present Soviets do not represent the will of the workers and peasants, immediately to re-elect the soviets by secret voting, with free preliminary agitation among all workers and peasants before the election.
2. Freedom of speech and press for workers, peasants, Anarchists and Left Socialist Parties.
3. Freedom of meetings, trade unions and peasant associations . . .
5. To liberate all political prisoners of Socialist Parties, and also workers, peasants, soldiers and sailors who have been imprisoned in connection with working class and peasant movements . . .
11. To grant the peasant full right to do what he sees fit with his land and also to possess cattle, which he must maintain and manage with his own strength, but without employing hired labour.

These demands were rejected by the Government and "Red Kronstadt" was brutally suppressed. It was done with regret and Trotsky was said to have been haunted to the end of his life by his part in the affair.

Other communists, including Lenin himself, were convinced that dictatorship was a regrettable necessity. Perhaps the last word should rest with a foreigner, Victor Serge, who had voluntarily emigrated to Russia to join in the great new socialist experiment:

After many hesitations, and with unutterable anguish, my Communist friends and I finally declared ourselves on the side of the Party. This is why. Kronstadt had right on its side. Kronstadt was the beginning of a fresh, liberating revolution for popular democracy. . . . However, the country was absolutely exhausted, and production practically at a standstill; there were no reserves of any kind, not even reserves of stamina in the hearts of the masses. . . . If the Bolshevik dictatorship fell, it was only a short step to chaos, and through chaos to a peasant rising, the massacre of Communists, the return of the emigres, and in the end, through the sheer force of events, another dictatorship, this time anti-proletarian.

(*Source:* V. Serge, *Memoirs of a Revolutionary*, London, 1967)

Sources

The principal first-hand sources of evidence of the attitudes and opinions that helped to make up the pattern of events in 1917 are the numerous newspapers that flourished after censorship was abolished in March of that year, the debates of the Provisional Government and the Soviet, and petitions, letters, speeches, etc, that arrived in the capital from the ordinary people of Russia. While access to these sources in the Soviet archives is difficult but not impossible, the main obstacle facing the English student of Russian history is the language barrier. Those who do not read Russian are forced to rely on those sources that appear in translation and thus have been selected by someone else. It is essential, therefore, always to be aware of any possible bias the author or editor may have.

The material quoted in this book has been drawn entirely from English-language sources.

NEWSPAPERS

Extracts available in translation have been quoted from:
Pravda ("Truth") and *Soldatskaya Pravda* ("Soldiers' Truth"): both Bolshevik papers.
Isvestia ("News"): Official mouthpiece of the Petrograd Soviet Ex-Com, expressing the Menshevik line and supporting the Coalition Government after May 1917.
Novaya Zhizn ("New Life"): Newspaper of the left-wing Menshevik Internationalists, opposing bourgeois-socialist coalition but hostile to Bolsheviks.
Ruskii Vedomosti ("Russian Truth"); *Rech* ("Speech"); and *Vestnik Partii Narodnoi Svobody* ("Herald of the Party of People's Freedom"): All three Kadet publications, critical of the Tsar before 1917; supporters of orderly government, a continuation of the war, postponement of economic reforms until after the war.
Soldat-Grazhdanin ("Citizen Soldier"): Newspaper produced by soldiers at the front; reflected views of rank and file.

COLLECTIONS OF DOCUMENTS

The Provisional Government 1917, 3 vols., R. Browder and A. Kerensky (Stanford, 1961): Compiled by the ex-Prime Minister to justify the policy of his administration and show the difficulties under which it laboured. Plenty of anti-Bolshevik opinion included but little about grass-roots aspirations.

The Bolshevik Revolution 1917-18. Documents and Materials, J. Bunyan and H. Fisher (Stanford, 1934): Balanced collection.

From the Red Archives, C. Vulliamy (London, 1929): Items released by the new Bolshevik government 1917-8 from the archives of the Tsarist and Provisional Governments. Designed to incriminate their enemies. Useful but unbalanced.

Lenin's Collected Works – selected, 8 vols., V. Lenin (Moscow 1936-9): The most usable English language selection of a vital source for understanding what the Bolsheviks did and why.

CONTEMPORARY ACCOUNTS

The problem of bias means that these must always be used with caution and, where possible, cross-checked with other sources.

An Ambassador's Memoirs, M. Paleologue (London, 1973): Diary of the French ambassador who recorded much that was being said in conservative and liberal circles between 1914 and May 1917. His own comments reflect the prejudices of his class and time.

Ten Days that Shook the World, J. Reed (London, 1970): Hour-by-hour account of Petrograd between 6 and 16 November by an American reporter who elbowed his way into all the important meetings and mixed freely on the streets. His interpretation of events is pro-Bolshevik, but his account of what was said and done accords well with other versions of the same period. An enthralling read.

Days, V. Shulgin (1925): Diary of liberal conservative reflecting the distaste felt for violent revolution from below.

The Russian Revolution of 1917: A Personal Record, N. Sukhanov (O.U.P. 1955): Detailed, eye-witness account of what was said, done and felt in Petrograd revolutionary circles.

LATER HISTORIES

The Russian Revolution, 2 vols, W.H. Chamberlin (New York, 1965): Written in 1930s by an American whose interest in the history of Russia was aroused when he lived there as Russian correspondent of the *Christian Science Monitor* and who called upon all the Soviet sources then available. A balanced study whose main conclusions have not really been upset by more recent research.

The Russian Revolution of February 1917, M. Ferro (London, 1972) *October 1917. A Social History of the Russian Revolution*, M. Ferro (London, 1980): Two invaluable studies, drawing on soviet archival material to paint a vivid picture of how workers, peasants and soldiers actually felt. Widely used in compiling this book.

The End of the Russian Empire, M. Florinsky (Yale U.P., 1961): Written in 1931, this book attempts to do the same as Ferro for the years 1914-17, but with much less archival material at hand. Nevertheless, it is a vivid account of what ordinary Russians felt about the war and an antidote to over-concentration on what the politicians said.

The History of the Russian Revolution, L. Trotsky (1932-3): Detailed account of 1917 by a Bolshevik participant. Full of useful material but cannot be relied upon to be objective.

Biographies

KAMENEV Lev B. (real name: Rosenfeld) (1883-1936): Bolshevik
Educated at the Law Faculty of Moscow University, from which he was expelled for revolutionary activities, Kamenev was the first senior Bolshevik to reach Petrograd from exile in 1917. Until Lenin's return he acted as party leader and editor of *Pravda*. Although he had supported Lenin's line before 1917, he publicly criticized the April Theses and argued that the November coup was "premature". In spite of his doubts, he remained in the Bolshevik Party, becoming one of Lenin's three deputies after the latter's stroke in 1922. During the 1920s and '30s he put up an intermittent resistance to Lenin's successor, Stalin, and was shot as a traitor after a show trial in 1936.

KERENSKY Alexander F. (1886-1970): Prime Minister of Russia July-November 1917
The son of a headmaster from the Volga town of Simbirsk (now Ulyanovsk), who had counted among his pupils the young Lenin, Kerensky became a lawyer and a Socialist Revolutionary deputy to the 4th Duma 1912-17. In March 1917 he was the only socialist to take office under the First Provisional Government. As government popularity waned, Kerensky, who was a brilliant orator, achieved ever-higher office – Minister for War in May, Prime Minister in July, Supreme Commander in Chief in September – in a vain attempt to win back popular support. As his policies were essentially the same as those of other socialist and liberal ministers, this stratagem was unsuccessful, and by November Kerensky's government was hated by the masses and despised by the generals.

When his attempt to retake Petrograd with troops from the front failed, Kerensky sneaked out of Russia on a false passport with the aid of a British secret service agent and spent the rest of his life in exile in France and the United States. He became the author of numerous books and articles explaining and justifying the activities of his government.

KORNILOV Lavr G. (1870-1918): Tsarist General
The son of a Cossack farmer, Kornilov had broken through the class barriers of the Imperial army to become the commander of an elite corps, the Savage Division. He was prepared to tolerate the February Revolution if the new Republican government could prove itself more capable of fighting a successful war than the old Tsarist one had been. Disillusioned by the failure of the July offensive, he persuaded himself that the Provisional Government *could* restore army morale if only it had the will, and this naive belief lay behind the so-called "Kornilov Affair" (see p.53). Imprisoned under comfortable conditions in a monastery at Bykhov, Kornilov escaped after the Bolshevik Revolution and found his way to General Alekseev in the south. As a commander of the Volunteer Army, he was killed by a shell at the storming of Bolshevik-held Ekaterinodar in April 1918.

LENIN Vladimir I. (1870-1924): Bolshevik
Son of an inspector of schools in Simbirsk, the young Lenin was much influenced by the execution of his elder brother for participating in a plot to assassinate Tsar Alexander II. As a student in the late 1880s he became a Marxist and spent most of the years between 1897 and 1917 in exile. He developed his own version of Marxism, now known in the Soviet Union as Marxism-Leninism, and created the Bolshevik Party, a tightly-knit group of revolutionaries who accepted Lenin's vision of the future.

On his return to Russia in 1917, Lenin immediately sensed that the radical mood of the Russian people could be made to work in his favour. With the support of his erstwhile rival, Trotsky, he set about making the bid for power that is the story of this book and died in January 1924 as the undisputed ruler of Soviet Russia.

NICHOLAS II (1868-1918): Last Tsar of Russia
A patriot with a sincere love of his country, charming in his private life, Nicholas II was reactionary in politics and weak in character. Determined to pass on to his son the absolute monarchy he had inherited from his father, he failed to see that the Russian monarchy could only survive if it made real concessions to the social and political forces of the 20th century. Nicholas' stifling of the Duma granted in 1905, his refusal to involve the middle classes in the running of the war and his failure to realize the strain that total war would impose on Russia's backward economy have been covered on pages 17-31. Moreover, in 1915 the Tsar appointed himself Commander in Chief of the army and left the day-to-day running of the government to the Tsarina Alexandra, who herself was under the influence of Rasputin, a charismatic and disreputable holy man. Convinced in March 1917 that abdication would be in the country's best interests, Nicholas accepted the consequences with resignation, perhaps even with relief. Placed under arrest, he was executed with the rest of his family at Ekaterinburg in the Urals in the summer of 1918.

TROTSKY Leon D. (real name Bronstein) (1879-1940): Bolshevik
The son of a landowner, Trotsky's earliest political experience was in organizing a strike in the Black Sea port of Nikolayev. This was rapidly followed by a period of exile in Siberia. Escaping abroad, he played a prominent part in Russian exile politics and devised his own theory of revolutionary progress. Like Lenin, he argued that Russia could move straight from autocracy to a workers' state, bypassing the bourgeois era, but only if the revolution in Russia were rapidly followed by socialist revolutions in the more industrialized European nations, thus cancelling out Russia's backwardness. This was the theory of *permanent revolution*.

1917 found Trotsky in the United States. Returning to Russia in May, he concluded that his politics and those of Lenin coincided, and the two became close collaborators. It was Trotsky who masterminded the military details of the October Revolution in Petrograd and whose organizational ability created the Red Army out of the amateur Red Guard. Although there were many differences between the two men, he remained Lenin's right-hand man until the latter's death in 1924. In the second half of the 1920s, however, Trotsky was outmanoeuvred by Stalin and exiled from the Soviet Union in 1929. In 1940 he was assassinated in Mexico by a Stalinist agent.

Glossary

All-Russian Congress of Soviets Congress of delegates from soviets all over Russia. The first convened on 16 June, the second on 7 November

Allies Russia's allies in the First World War – Britain, France and (from April 1917) the U.S.A.

ataman traditional Cossack chieftain

Baltic Provinces states of Latvia, Lithuania and Estonia, which were part of the Russian Empire until 1918

bourgeoisie the property-owning middle class

Cain biblical character, who betrayed and killed his brother

capitalist believer in a free-enterprise economy. Marxists believed that the capitalist economic system was typical of the bourgeois stage of development that would precede socialism

Central Committee representatives from the main party organizations all over Russia. Decision-making body of the Bolshevik Party

collectivized agriculture amalgamation of individual farms into larger one worked in common by a number of families; may be done voluntarily or by the state

Cossacks peoples inhabiting Don and Kuban areas of southern Russia; traditional elite troops of the Tsarist Empire

Death battalions elite fighting regiments of the Tsarist army

demagogy a technique by which a politician wins support by appealing to people's emotions and prejudices, rather than to their reason and understanding

democracy i) a system of government in which supreme power is held by the will of the people
ii) applied by Russian socialists in 1917 to government by the will of the working and peasant classes only. Other Russian classes were excluded from the definition

Duma Russian parliament, established 1905

Emperor Wilhelm William II, German Emperor 1888-1918; Russia's opponent in First World War

Ex-Com the Executive Committee of the Petrograd Soviet, responsible for running its day-to-day affairs, representing the opinion of the Soviet to the Provisional Government and editing *Isvestia*

fraternization refusal of troops of warring armies to fight each other; rather they mingle as brothers or friends

Kadets Russian political party of the middle class

Kronstadt naval base in the Gulf of Finland near Petrograd; hotbed of Bolshevism 1917

Left Socialist Revolutionaries radical wing of SRs, who sided with Bolsheviks in November 1917

Lettish from Latvia

October Manifesto proclamation by Tsar Nicholas II granting a Duma, October 1905

Octobrists Russian political party of the upper middle class

People's Commissars ministers of the Bolshevik government

pood Russian measurement of weight, equivalent to 36 English lbs.

Pugachev leader of a violent peasant uprising, 1773

Red Guard Bolshevik militia recruited in the factories, 1917

Romanov family name of the Tsars of Russia

rouble Russian monetary unit. 100 kopecks = 1 rouble

Russian Poland an area of Poland with Warsaw as its capital that was part of the Russian Empire until 1918

sahzen land measurement equivalent to 7 English feet

soviet i) popularly elected council; played a large part in events of 1917
ii) adjective describing anything connected with the Soviet Union, the name of the Russian state after 1917

speculator someone who buys commodities cheaply, then hoards them until the price rises

St Petersburg the name by which Petrograd, the Russian capital, was known before 1914. Now Leningrad

Tauride Palace meeting-place of the Petrograd Soviet, 1917

Tsarist Empire pre-1917 Russian state, stretching from Finland in the north to the Black Sea in the south, and from Warsaw in the west to Vladivostok in the east. Included over 80 different nationalities

universal suffrage one man, one vote

westernization bringing Russia in line with western Europe, especially in fields of industrialization and parliamentary institutions

zemstvo elected local council of Tsarist Russia

Index